PACKED

PACKED

Lunch hacks and recipes to squeeze
more nutrients into your day

Becky Alexander & Michelle Lake

NOURISH

EAT WELL, LIVE WELL

Dedication: For everyone who's had enough of cheese sandwiches

Packed

Becky Alexander and Michelle Lake

First published in the UK and USA in 2017 by Nourish, an imprint of Watkins Media Limited
19 Cecil Court
London WC2N 4EZ

enquiries@nourishbooks.com

Managing Editor: Rebecca Woods
Editor: Jan Cutler
Art Direction: Georgina Hewitt
Design: Geoff Borin
Production: Beata Kibil
Commissioned Photography: Haarala Hamilton
Food Stylist: Rebecca Woods
Prop Stylist: Wei Tang

A CIP record for this book is available from the British Library

ISBN: 978-1-84899-315-0

10 9 8 7 6 5 4 3 2 1

Typeset in Source Sans Pro and Cookies&Milk

Colour reproduction by XY Digital
Printed in China

Publisher's note:
While every care has been taken in compiling the recipes for this book, Watkins Media Limited, or any other persons who have been involved in working on this publication, cannot accept responsibility for any errors or omissions, inadvertent or not, that may be found in the recipes or text, nor for any problems that may arise as a result of preparing one of these recipes. If you are pregnant or breastfeeding or have any special dietary requirements or medical conditions, it is advisable to consult a medical professional before following any of the recipes contained in this book.

Notes:
Unless otherwise stated:
• Use medium fruit and vegetables
• Use fresh ingredients, including herbs and spices
• Do not mix imperial and metric measurements.

 1 teaspoon = 5ml
 1 tablespoon = 15ml
 1 cup = 240ml

nourishbooks.com

CONTENTS

INTRODUCTION

BECKY: This is the book I needed about 20 years ago when I started work. My first proper job was for a magazine based on an industrial estate where you had to take your lunch with you or live on dodgy bacon rolls. I got very bored with sandwiches. I have worked in London for many years since then, and our options have got a hundred times better in that time: you can buy vegan, sushi, gluten-free, green juices, chia porridge … anything you want. I have done all that, but a while ago I realized that lots of the takeout options cost a lot for what they are and they can be on the mean side (half an egg, anyone?). Queuing up for your lunch is boring and doesn't feel like a break.

You will find lots of ideas in this book that will give you a delicious lunch without hassle and for a sensible price. No one has hours to spend making lunch in the morning, so the ideas are quick, realistic and you can take them on the train, tube/subway or bus. And all the recipes are packed with nutrition, which is where Michelle comes in . . .

MICHELLE: In the past 10 years since I set up Mission Nutrition, my nutritional therapy practice, I've helped countless clients take control of their own diet and reach their personal health goals. Lunch is always the meal they struggle with the most. Lack of time and inspiration, shift work and travel are all factors. All sorts of professionals come through my door: air stewards, paramedics, teachers, social workers, doctors, business people, police officers and commuters, to name a few, and I've devised lots of really practical and portable breakfasts, lunches and snack ideas to fit into their busy schedules.

It's so rewarding when clients tell me how much better they feel after a few weeks of eating a new nourishing diet. A little effort, planning and a list of good ideas can dramatically improve anyone's health and energy levels.

I was delighted when Becky asked me to work with her on this book so that I could share my nutrition experience with more people. I thoroughly believe that food should look and taste delicious as well as being good for you, and all our recipe ideas are not only healthy and nutrition packed, but they taste really great too.

WHAT MAKES A GREAT LUNCH?

Lunch should help you feel recharged and ready to take on whatever the afternoon has to throw at you. However busy you are, you deserve to eat well and take the time to nourish yourself. Far too many of us skip lunch, eat the same things every day or eat poor-quality food, and this can mean that we just don't get the variety of nutrients our body requires. If you feel an energy slump at 4pm and 'need' a snack, you probably are just not eating what your body requires at lunchtime.

NO WEIRD INGREDIENTS

There is an amazing amount of rubbish in the food sold today. Additives, fillers, bulking agents, extra salt – even some healthy-sounding foods can contain things we don't want to eat, such as sugar in yogurt and muesli. Making your own means you know exactly what's in there. You can make sure the eggs are free-range, there is no mayo in your sandwich, and you know how fresh the food is. When buying packs of bread, crackers, cookies or cakes, look out for hydrogenated fats and trans-fats. These are processed fats that are no good for anybody; the body finds them difficult to process and there are links to cancer.

VALUE FOR MONEY

We are not anti spending money on lunch. You need to eat. What we do mind is paying over the odds for sandwiches, soups and salads made with low-quality ingredients that aren't giving you the nutrition you need. Add up what you are spending each day/week/month on lunch, coffee and snacks. For this you can buy a lot of fantastic ingredients to make the lunches in the book. You might save enough to spend on a weekend away, tickets for something, or a great meal out at the end of the month – whatever motivates you.

MIX THINGS UP

Buying your lunch from the same outlets every day means that you could be eating a fairly limited range of foods. Even if you already pack your own lunch, it's easy to slip into a rut (tuna sandwich every day?). Here's what you get from a *Packed* lunch, breakfast or snack:

1 **Carbohydrates**, but the right ones. Eating refined carbs such as white bread, rice or pasta causes blood sugar to shoot up dramatically. The pancreas releases insulin to rapidly bring it down again. At this point you'll be feeling tired, irritable and less focused – ready to grab a sugary snack to boost your energy again. All our ideas are based on low-glycaemic load (GL) carbohydrates that supply you with a slow release of fuel to keep you going throughout the day. Oats, wholegrain breads, brown rice, beans, lentils, pulses and sweet potatoes will all keep you off the energy rollercoaster.

2 **Good-quality protein** to give you energy and keep you full for the afternoon ahead. Nuts, beans, pulses, meat, fish, eggs, cheese and seeds all add to your protein intake, and the more variety, the better.

3 **Lots of veggies.** Did you know that we should eat at least seven portions of vegetables and fruit a day? And that only two of those should be fruit? Aim to make at least half of your lunch veggies. Salads are an obvious way to eat them, but soups, stews and dips count too. Add salad to your sandwiches, or eat a salad or soup alongside. It's good advice to 'eat the rainbow': aim for a range of colours in the fruit and veg you buy to get all the different nutrients. As a very rough guide, one serving can fit into your hand.

4 **Some healthy fats.** Fats are a super source of energy and are essential to help absorb the nutrients found in many plant foods. We've used lots of ingredients rich in amazing omega oils throughout our recipes. The omega-3s have been shown to increase focus and concentration – important when you are working hard. You'll find them in oily fish, flaxseeds, pumpkin seeds and walnuts. For skin, heart and hormone health, look to the omega-6 and -9 fats found in nuts, seeds and olive oil.

Even butter is back on the menu and has been shown to be better for you than processed spreads and margarines; just don't eat lots of it. We recommend rapeseed/canola oil for cooking, as it contains omega-3, -6 and -9 fats and doesn't become harmful when heated. Ideally, choose a cold-pressed or extra virgin rapeseed oil. It is also a rich source of skin and heart-friendly vitamin E.

Coconut oil is great for both baking and frying, and is a useful dairy-free alternative to butter. Use extra virgin coconut oil, or if you're not keen on the taste, buy a good-quality coconut butter (make sure it doesn't contain any hydrogenated fat).

PLAN AHEAD AND SAVE TIME

No one has hours to spend making elaborate lunches. Most ideas in this book are made with ingredients you can pull out of the cupboard or freezer, or that last for most of the week in the fridge.

1 **Do an online shop at the weekend.** With early and late deliveries, no petrol or parking costs, it is a no-brainer. If you don't buy enough each week, do it once a fortnight. Once you have a basic list online, it takes just minutes to re-order. Order plenty of pulses, nuts, cans of fish, olives, roast veggies, frozen fruit, feta, etc. ready to make a lunch.

2 **Buying online means you get a wider range of ingredients** than at the local shop. You'll save money, too, as you won't buy random or hunger-driven things that you don't need.

3 **If you have a freezer**, buy frozen chopped garlic, ginger, chilli, butternut squash, peas and spinach. That's a curry right there. Buy bags of frozen berries too, for smoothies and quick desserts.

4 **Buy a delicious loaf of bread**, cut it into wedges, and freeze it so that you have something lovely to eat, rather than long-life ready sliced.

5 **Buy veggies, fruits and herbs** that last for ages. Rocket/arugula and spinach will last all week in the fridge (softer leaves won't). A pot of mint will last for weeks but some soft herbs like coriander/cilantro won't.

6 **When a recipe says it makes enough for two,** the second portion will last a couple of days in the fridge, either at home or tucked away in the office fridge. Or you can share it.

7 **If you don't have everything listed in the recipe,** miss it out or add something else; don't be put off. Herbs are lovely but optional every time.

8 **Look out for these 3 symbols to help you to get organized:**

Make ahead: recipes that you can make at the weekend, and will last for a few days.

Freezes well: soups, stews and snacks that will freeze well so you always have something to grab on busy days.

Super quick: ideas that can be thrown together in 5 minutes or less; as quick as making a sandwich.

HEALTHY HACKS

There are a few things you can do right away to cram more goodness into your lunch:

1 Use yogurt instead of mayonnaise in sandwiches. Yogurt will give you a good shot of friendly bacteria to boost your tummy health, plus you'll know exactly what you're eating. Many shop-bought mayonnaises contain a whole list of unwanted ingredients including sugar. Yogurt is fab with chicken, turkey and fish (see pages 145–7).

2 Try pesto in your sandwich instead of butter. Make home-made pesto with leaves and herbs from the fridge (see Summer Garden Sandwich on page 151), and use in sandwiches for a big dose of green goodness.

3 Stop eating pasta salads; they play havoc with your blood sugar levels. Instead, spiralize veggies like courgette/zucchini to use as a base for salads to get heaps more nutrients.

4 Use dried fruit or fruit purée to add sweetness to snacks. You'll get a double whammy of fibre and nutrients that you won't get from refined sugar.

PACKING YOUR LUNCH

Invest in one or two new lunch boxes that are dishwasher-proof and that will fit in your work fridge. One with compartments is handy for dips, sushi and deli plates (see pages 154–5). You will also need a couple of mini ice packs to keep everything cool; you won't even need a work fridge if you use an insulated lunch bag.

For salads, we love jars with clip-on lids so that you can see the delicious ingredients as you layer them up. Plastic shaker pots are good too, and are lighter to carry around.

Insulated food flasks are perfect for keeping hot food hot. Warm your flask with boiling water, then pour away the water and add your hot porridge/oatmeal, soup or stew; it will be perfect at lunchtime, with no need for a blast from a microwave. Eat straight from the flask or decant it into a bowl, if you have a good supply at work.

★ PACKED WITH . . .

Packing your own lunch gives you the opportunity to try lots of different foods you might not have thought about. Look out for the 'Packed With . . .' boxes with each recipe that tell you what nutrients are packed into your lunch and how they can supercharge your health.

LOOKING AFTER YOURSELF AT LUNCH

If you want to improve your health and wellbeing, you can't afford to let the food you eat during the working day let you down. Studies show that when people don't take a proper lunch break, they feel less productive in the afternoon, make more mistakes and feel more stressed. You might think you are getting more done by skipping lunch, but you are probably making yourself less useful in the afternoon. Being better nourished should mean fewer sick days too.

There are quick breakfast ideas in Get Up and Go (see pages 16–43). Some of these can be prepped the night before such as Hot or Cold Overnight Oats (see page 30) or whizzed up quickly in the morning like the Berry Smoothie Bowl (see page 20). If you want to make a few breakfasts in advance try our Grab and Go Yogurt Pots (see page 28) or Coconut, Pistachio and Goji Berry Granola Bars (see page 39).

For delicious salad ideas crammed full of superfoods, dip into Salads and Slaws (see pages 44–89). When you want something warming, choose from Filling Flasks (see pages 90–125). Some of these soups and stew recipes are so simple that you can prepare them in the morning, such as Prawn Tom Yum Soup (see page 95) or Portable Noodles (see page 114–5), others you can batch-cook at the weekend. Go to Fork-Free Meals (pages 126–163) for easy and nutritious sushi, dip and sandwich ideas. And if you need healthy grazing ideas that do you good, go to Snacks and Bites (pages 164–185).

All our recipes and packing tips have been road-tested by our family and friends. We're confident that they taste fantastic and they also travel well. Each one has been carefully put together to give you the right mix of nutrients to keep you energized throughout the day and keep you fit and healthy in the long term.

What are you waiting for? It's time to revolutionize your lunchbox.

1. GET UP <u>AND</u> GO

Whizz up this protein- and fibre-rich smoothie for a satisfying and luscious start to the day.

BLACKBERRY, APPLE AND CINNAMON SMOOTHIE

1 medjool date, pitted

50g/1¾oz/heaped ⅓ cup frozen blackberries

½ eating apple, grated

½ tsp ground cinnamon

1 tsp almond butter

1 tsp ground flaxseed

200ml/7fl oz/scant 1 cup unsweetened almond milk, plus extra if needed

1 tbsp jumbo/rolled oats (optional)

MAKES 1 BREAKFAST

- Soak the date in boiling water while you gather together the remaining ingredients, then drain well.

- Put all the ingredients into a blender or food processor and whizz until smooth. If using rolled oats, add a little more almond milk or water, so that your smoothie doesn't become too thick. Pour into a sealable smoothie cup.

★ PACKED WITH . . .

Blackberries, with their dark blue colour, are particularly high in anthocyanins – antioxidants that help to keep the brain in tip-top condition. Cinnamon can be helpful in controlling blood sugar levels and reducing sweet cravings.

Eat this thick and fruity smoothie with a spoon for a vitamin C-packed breakfast. If you have a very powerful blender, you can make this straight from frozen, otherwise defrost the berries overnight in the fridge.

BERRY SMOOTHIE BOWL

100g/3½oz/scant 1 cup frozen raspberries

50g/1¾oz/scant ½ cup frozen blueberries

1 tsp ground flaxseed

1 tsp dried goji berries

1 tbsp Greek yogurt

MAKES 1 BREAKFAST

- Put all the ingredients into a blender or food processor and whizz together until smooth.

- Transfer to a lidded container and keep cool until you are ready to eat.

 TIP Look for bags of ready-milled seeds – just put a spoonful in your breakfast each day and you'll get easy extra nutrients.

Frozen berries are much cheaper than fresh, and having a few bags in the freezer means that this easy breakfast is always available to you, whatever the season.

★ PACKED WITH . . .

The protein in the yogurt and flaxseed will give you energy until lunchtime. As well as being a great plant source of omega-3 fatty acids, flaxseeds are fibre rich and will give your digestion a morning wake-up call. This breakfast is your fruit quota for the day (see page 11).

1   Think you need caffeine as soon as you wake
    up in the morning? It's just a habit. Drink plenty
    of water instead and maybe try a Hot Morning
    Zinger (see page 23) and see how you feel. Save
    coffee or tea for mid-morning once you've eaten
    and your body is hydrated.

2   Caffeine, like sugar, causes your blood sugar
    to rise and fall dramatically, setting you on a
    rollercoaster of irritation and hunger for the rest
    of the day. Think quality not quantity. Swigging
    mugs of tea and coffee throughout the day is an
    easy habit to fall into. Instead, treat yourself to
    one decent cup per day, then switch to water or
    herbal tea.

3   If you're going through a stressful time at work,
    you actually need less, not more, caffeine.
    Too much caffeine can rob you of energy and
    nutrients so that you can become anxious,
    stressed and less able to concentrate.

PIMP YOUR WATER BOTTLE

Do you drink enough water every day? There are no official guidelines as to how much you should drink, as it varies depending on your size, how active you are and the temperature. Basically, if you feel thirsty, lack energy in the afternoons or get frequent headaches, it's worth looking at your water intake. With so many soft drinks containing sugar, we've got some ideas to perk up good old tap water.

BOTTLE OR TAP?

If you care about the environment, opt for tap water; we don't need millions of plastic bottles going to waste. Plus, why line the pockets of multinational companies who are selling us something we can get for free in our own homes? If you live in a hard water area, use a filter jug to remove limescale and improve your water's taste. Or treat yourself to a new infusion water bottle; some filter tap water, and you can add interesting ingredients to the middle compartment to flavour your water and get added nutrients. The 800ml/28fl oz/3½ cup infuser bottle is a good size, and you can refill it at lunchtime.

SPARKLING OR STILL?

Sparkling water can make a refreshing alternative to still, is just as hydrating and it might feel like more of a treat. Too much sparkling water might give you a tummy ache, so don't go overboard. Some sparkling mineral waters are high in sodium, so check labels carefully. Anything with more than 20mg per litre/ 35fl oz should be avoided.

THINGS TO ADD

Lots of flavoured waters contain sugar, sweeteners and additives, sometimes as much as a can of cola. If you want to flavour good old tap water, there are loads of things you can add. Try these on their own or make up combinations: basil leaves, blackberries, blueberries, cucumber slices, grapefruit wedge, green tea bag, kiwi fruit slices, lemon slices, lime slices, orange slices, passionfruit, peach slices, raspberries, rooibos tea bag, rosemary sprig and slivers of watermelon.

HOT MORNING ZINGER

This warming combination of lemon, ginger, mint and cayenne pepper will start your day with a real kick. Save time by preparing it in a vacuum flask the night before. It will infuse nicely and you'll avoid an expensive visit to the coffee shop on the way to work.

MAKES 1 DRINK

Put the **juice of ½ lemon** in a vacuum flask and add **2cm/¾in piece of peeled root ginger**, **2–3 mint sprigs**, to taste, and a **pinch of cayenne pepper**. Pour in **500ml/17fl oz/2 cups boiling water**. Give the flask a gentle shake, and sip now or seal and take to work.

★ PACKED WITH . . . This combination of citrus, mint and spices wakes up your liver, kick starts the digestive system and rehydrates your cells.

CUCUMBER AND MINT INFUSION

Just a few slices of cucumber and mint leaves add a refreshing flavour to water.

MAKES 1 DRINK

Slice **2.5cm/1in cucumber** and put into the central compartment of your infusion water bottle with a **few mint leaves**. Fill the bottle with **ice-cold water**. By the time you get to work the flavours will have infused.

★ PACKED WITH . . . This gives you a healthy shot of water-soluble vitamin C. Eat the cucumber once you've finished to get a dose of skin-friendly silica.

This fresh-tasting salad, made with low-glycaemic-load fruit, is bursting with flavour and health benefits. Matcha green tea powder has a delicate bitterness that goes well with sweet fruit. It is quite pricey, but you only need to use a little at a time.

SUPERFRUIT WITH MATCHA, YOGURT ᴀɴᴅ PISTACHIOS

1 papaya, peeled, pitted and chopped

150g/5½oz/heaped 1 cup blueberries

100g/3½oz pomegranate seeds (see Tip on page 66)

2 passion fruits, cut in half

1 tsp matcha green tea powder

125g/4½oz/heaped ½ cup Greek or coconut yogurt

4 tsp pistachio nuts, shelled

MAKES 4 BREAKFASTS

• Put the papaya, blueberries and pomegranate seeds in a large dish. Scoop out the seedy pulp from the passion fruits into the bowl and stir gently to combine.

• Mix the matcha with 1 teaspoon cold water to form a paste, and stir into the yogurt until well combined.

• Spoon a quarter of the fruit salad into a small sealable jar or pot. Top with a quarter of the yogurt and sprinkle over 1 teaspoon pistachios. Seal the jar.

• Keep cold until ready to eat. This salad keeps well for 4 days in the fridge, depending on the freshness of the fruit, so you can eat it over a few days.

★ PACKED WITH . . .

Matcha tea is cultivated to be super-high in antioxidants. It has a milder and fresher taste than regular green tea. Although it does contain caffeine, it tends to induce a calm focus rather than the twitchy buzz from coffee.

Papaya contains the enzyme papain, which breaks down proteins and eases inflammation in the body. Papaya is also brimming with beta-carotene and vitamin C, crucial for the immune system. Pomegranate and passion fruit seeds are crammed with antioxidants and vitamin C.

You can find yogurt pots in lots of coffee shops and supermarkets, so why make your own? Well, the mark-up is amazing for a start. You can buy better quality ingredients for the same price, plus you can add a decent amount of fruit, seeds and nuts rather than the scattering that the shops add. Most bought pots won't give you enough energy to last you until lunch, but by making your own you can give yourself a breakfast packed with nutrition. Make two or three of these pots at a time to last a few days. Use a sealable jar or pot and your yogurt will be easy to take to work.

GRAB AND GO YOGURT POTS

YOGURT FACTS

• Buy a large pot of yogurt labelled 'live' or with 'active cultures' to get the probiotic benefits (see below).

• Check product labels carefully – not all yogurt is good for you. A well-made yogurt doesn't need added ingredients such as sugar, artificial sweeteners, additives or thickeners, such as pectin or guar gum. Yogurt should just contain milk and live bacteria, nothing else. Buy pots of plain yogurt and add your own fruit for sweetness.

• If you're feeling low, yogurt might help. It's a good source of the mood-boosting amino acid tryptophan.

• Buy full-fat yogurt, never low-fat or fat-free. Full fat is far more satisfying and contains the fat-soluble antioxidant vitamins A and E, which are both fab for your eyes and skin. Low-fat yogurts usually contain loads of added sugar.

• Greek yogurt is our first choice for pots. It is strained more thoroughly than plain yogurt to give it a thicker, creamier texture, making it a good base.

• Mix things up. Try coconut yogurt, which provides plenty of beneficial bacteria as well as fibre and vitamins. Soy yogurt tends to contain artificial thickeners and preservatives, so it isn't the best option.

★ PACKED WITH . . .

Yogurt is made by adding two bacterial cultures (*Lactobacillus bulgaricus* and *Streptococcus thermophilus*) to milk. This fermenting process gives yogurt its flavour and creamy texture. It also makes it great for your gut and immune system. Yogurt is also a great source of calcium for healthy bones and teeth.

Use a sealable jar or pot, and fill it full of delicious yogurt, fruit, nuts and seeds. If you like, mix the seeds with the yogurt first, before layering.

BREAKFAST LAYER POT

2 tbsp Fig, Apricot and
   Prune Compote (see
   below) or berries

2 tbsp yogurt

1 tsp chopped almonds
   or pistachio nuts

1 tsp pumpkin, black
   sesame or chia seeds

MAKES 1 BREAKFAST

• Put 1 tablespoon of the compote into a sealable jar or pot. Follow with 1 tablespoon of the yogurt, then another tablespoon of compote. Add a layer of nuts and another 1 tablespoon yogurt, then, finally, top with the seeds.

This easy compote smells and tastes amazing, and it is so much cheaper than any you could buy. Make a pot of this and dip into it throughout the week. It is lovely on top of porridge/oatmeal as well as with yogurt.

FIG, APRICOT AND PRUNE COMPOTE

5 dried figs, chopped

5 dried apricots, chopped

5 pitted dried dates, chopped

5 prunes, chopped

1 small cinnamon stick

1 tsp frozen chopped ginger
   or 1cm/½in piece of root
   ginger, peeled and grated

zest and juice of 1 orange

MAKES 5 SERVINGS

• Put the figs, apricots, dates and prunes in a small saucepan. Add the cinnamon stick, ginger, orange zest and juice and 200ml/7fl oz/scant 1 cup water. Cover and bring to the boil. Reduce the heat and simmer for 20 minutes or until the liquid is syrupy and the fruit is softened. Remove the cinnamon stick. Leave to cool. Store in the fridge in an airtight container for up to 1 week.

Soaking rolled oats the night before means that this breakfast only takes a minute to pull together in the morning. Cold overnight oats are delicious and taste a little like rice pudding.

HOT OR COLD OVERNIGHT OATS

50g/1¾oz/½ cup jumbo/ rolled oats

1 tbsp chia seeds

125ml/4fl oz/½ cup unsweetened almond or soy milk

1 tbsp Greek yogurt

MAKES 1 BREAKFAST

- Tip the oats and chia seeds into a bowl or sealable jar, and give them a quick stir. Pour in the milk and yogurt, and stir again. Cover and put in the fridge overnight.

- In the morning, add whatever topping you like, and take to work to eat cold as it is. Alternatively, for a hot breakfast, tip the mixture into a saucepan and heat it through for 1 minute until hot. You might need to add a little water to loosen. Transfer to a vacuum food flask, add your toppings, seal and eat it later at work.

PORRIDGE/OATMEAL TOPPINGS Add a variety of fruits, seeds and nuts each time you make this so that you have a range of vitamins and nutrients: a few pistachio nuts or chopped almonds, a handful of fresh blueberries or raspberries (add frozen berries the night before so that they can defrost), dried goji berries, sliced banana or sultanas/ golden raisins. Top with a few pumpkin seeds.

★ PACKED WITH . . .

Oats are so good for you – they are a filling source of soluble fibre known as beta-glucan, which helps to maintain healthy cholesterol levels. Soaking allows the starch to break down making digestion easier. Eaten cold, the resistant-starch content of your oats is increased so you'll feel fuller for longer than eating hot porridge/oatmeal.

If you already love porridge/oatmeal, try this variation. Quinoa gives it a lighter texture and adds extra nutrients to your breakfast. Soaking the mixture overnight saves you cooking time in the morning, and the sultanas/golden raisins will start to plump up. Just a few sultanas/golden raisins provide all the sweetness you need.

QUINOA, OATS AND CHIA PORRIDGE

300ml/10½fl oz/1¼ cups unsweetened soy, almond or cow's milk (or half milk: half water)

25g/1oz/¼ cup quinoa flakes

25g/1oz/¼ cup jumbo/rolled oats

1 tsp ground chia seeds

1 tbsp sultanas/golden raisins

MAKES 1 BREAKFAST

- Measure out the milk into a measuring jug/pitcher, and add all the remaining ingredients. Stir well.

- Cover the jug with cling film/plastic wrap and put in the fridge overnight.

- In the morning, pour the mixture into a saucepan and heat through until bubbling. Cook for 2–3 minutes until the quinoa and oats have absorbed all the liquid and you like the consistency. To take to work, pour into a vacuum food flask.

◤ TIME TO EAT ◥ If you've left the porridge/oatmeal for a couple of hours, add a little boiling water and mix well to loosen it before eating, if you need to.

★ PACKED WITH . . .

As a seed, quinoa is much higher in protein than grain foods, so it keeps you fuller for longer. It provides the whole range of B vitamins, especially B_5, which helps us to handle stress better.

Making your own muesli is better value than buying a box, and you can avoid raisins, coconut, nuts or whatever it is you usually pick out. You can also skip the added sugar and syrup coating that can go into shop-bought mueslis. Feel free to use your favourite nuts, seeds, fruit and flakes to mix it up a bit.

MUESLI MADE EASY

100g/3½oz/1 cup jumbo/ rolled oats

100g/3½oz/1 cup spelt flakes

50g/1¾oz/⅓ cup whole dried apricots, snipped into pieces

50g/1¾oz/scant ½ cup blanched whole hazelnuts

50g/1¾oz/heaped ⅓ cup sunflower seeds

1 tbsp whole black chia seeds

milk or orange juice, to serve

MAKES 5 BREAKFASTS

- Put the oats and spelt in a large mixing bowl. Add the apricots, hazelnuts, sunflower seeds and chia seeds, and mix well.

- Transfer the muesli to an airtight container. It will keep for at least 2 weeks.

TIME TO EAT Measure out about 85g/3oz/¾ cup of muesli into a bowl, and pour over milk or orange juice.

MIX IT UP
Hate hazelnuts? Love dried cherries? Need to eat gluten-free? Just follow the quantities above and swap for your favourite ingredients to make your perfect muesli. It's probably best not to add lots more dried fruit because the recommended daily amount is only 30g/1oz/2 tbsp.

Here are some ideas:
Nuts: almonds, Brazil nuts, pecan nuts, walnuts
Flakes: barley, buckwheat, coconut, quinoa, rye
Dried fruit: apple, apricot, banana, blackcurrants, blueberries, cherries, cranberries, dates, pineapple, sultanas/golden raisins
Seeds: chia, flaxseed, pumpkin, sunflower

★ PACKED WITH . . .

The seeds and hazelnuts in this muesli will give you some protein, which will help to give you energy until lunchtime. Chia seeds are a great source of omega-3 fats.

GOOD-FOR-YOU GRANOLA

Most shop-bought granola is eye-wateringly high in fat and sugar, and is far from a healthy start to the day. It's simple to make a nutritious granola, and there are endless delicious combinations (it's a great way to use up some storecupboard ingredients, for example). Granola differs from muesli because most of the ingredients have been toasted to form crunchy clusters. Homemade granola also makes a healthy snack – just pop a handful into a small tub to nibble in the afternoon. By keeping added sugar to a minimum and throwing in plenty of protein-rich nuts and seeds, you get a granola with a low glycaemic load to deliver sustained energy until lunchtime.

⚑ PICK-AND-MIX GRANOLA ⚑

MAKES 5 BREAKFASTS

Pick one thing from each section to make a balanced breakfast:

Preheat the oven to 150°C/300°F/gas 2. Heat the fat over a low heat in a large non-stick saucepan. Add the sweetener and stir until dissolved. Add the grains and spices, and stir well.

Spread the mixture over a large baking pan and bake for 45 minutes or until slightly golden and crunchy. Sprinkle the nuts and/or seeds over the mixture and cook for a further 5 minutes. Keep your eye on the mixture, as it can burn easily. Once cooled, put the granola into an airtight container and add your dried fruit. Shake gently to mix. It will keep well for up to 2 weeks.

Extra virgin coconut oil or butter works best to make good clusters. You could also replace 1 tbsp of the oil with 1 tbsp tahini or nut butter, such as peanut, almond or cashew (unsalted and unsweetened).

SWEETENER:

2 tbsp sweetener
You need something sticky to bring everything together and add crunch. You only need a little, however. Choose from honey, coconut sugar, maple syrup, apple purée or lucuma powder. (Peruvian lucuma fruit is nutrient-rich with a low-glycaemic load and an aromatic caramel-like flavour.)

GRAINS:

150g/5½oz grains (1½ cups of jumbo/rolled oats or 1 cup of quinoa flakes or buckwheat)
Rolled oats make a great base for granola, but if you're on a low-carb regime you can leave them out entirely. Quinoa or raw buckwheat are good low-carb options.

SPICES:

1 tbsp spice
A little extra flavour will make your granola delicious. Try grated nutmeg, ground cinnamon or mixed spice, and you could also try vanilla extract, orange zest and raw cacao powder or nibs.

NUTS:

1 tbsp nuts
Use a mix of flaked, chopped and whole nuts for a variety of textures. Almonds, Brazil nuts, hazelnuts, pecan nuts, pistachio nuts, walnuts, and coconut pieces all work well.

SEEDS:

2 tbsp seeds
Add flax or chia seeds for their omega-3 fats, and add after toasting to keep their amazing oils intact. You could also try poppy, pumpkin, sesame and sunflower seeds.

FRUIT:

1 tbsp dried fruit
Fruit adds sweetness and chewy contrast. Try unsweetened apple rings, apricots, blueberries, cherries, chopped dates, cranberries, dried goji berries, raisins, sultanas/golden raisins.

Easy to rustle up, these bars are a good option when you need to eat breakfast on the go or for an afternoon snack. Almond, cashew or macadamia nut butters all work well to add protein and flavour.

COCONUT, PISTACHIO AND GOJI BERRY GRANOLA BARS

100g/3½oz/1 cup jumbo/ rolled oats

50g/1¾oz/¼ cup extra virgin coconut oil

2 tbsp honey

2 tbsp nut butter (of choice)

1 tsp vanilla extract

3 tbsp raw, shelled pistachio nuts, roughly chopped

50g/1¾oz/⅔ cup desiccated coconut/ dried shredded coconut

2 tbsp dried goji berries

MAKES 8 BARS

- Preheat the oven to 180°C/350°F/gas 4. Line a 23 × 15cm/ 9 × 6in shallow baking pan with baking parchment. Spread the oats thinly over the parchment and bake for 15 minutes or until golden.

- Put the oil, honey, nut butter and vanilla extract in a saucepan over a medium-low heat, and heat gently until well combined and the oil is melted.

- Stir in the baked oats until well coated. Add the remaining ingredients and mix well.

- Tip the mixture back into the baking pan and press down firmly using damp hands.

- Put in the fridge for 1 hour or until firm, and then cut into 8 bars. Wrap each bar in parchment to take to work. Store in an airtight container for up to one week or freeze for up to 3 months. Defrost at room temperature for a couple of hours.

★ PACKED WITH . . .

Vibrant red and intensely flavoured, the tiny goji berry is rich in carotenoids and antioxidants that help to protect our eyes from damage. They are a little pricey, but they keep well and you only need to add a small amount to bars, porridge/oatmeal, granola or salads to reap their health benefits.

This is a grown-up muffin, totally unlike the sugar-filled muffins you can buy in coffee shops. The dates add a rich, sweet flavour that goes well with a cup of morning coffee.

DATE AND PECAN SPELT MUFFINS

200g/7oz/scant 1½ cups wholemeal/whole-wheat spelt flour

50g/1¾oz/½ cup jumbo/rolled oats

50g/1¾oz/¼ cup golden caster/superfine sugar

1 tsp baking powder

25g/1oz/scant ¼ cup pecan nuts, broken, plus 6 whole nuts for the tops

50g/1¾oz/⅓ cup pitted dried dates, chopped

2 eggs

150ml/5fl oz/scant ⅔ cup rapeseed/canola oil

1 banana, mashed

25ml/5 tsp milk, if needed

MAKES 6 MUFFINS

★ PACKED WITH . . .

Spelt is an ancient grain that is lower in gluten, and often easier to digest, than modern wheat. Combined with the oats, the spelt gives you a wider range of nutrients than you would have if you used processed white flour for the muffins, and the pecans and eggs provide some protein.

• Preheat the oven to 180°C/350°F/gas 4. Line a six-cup muffin pan with paper cases.

• Sieve/sift the flour into a mixing bowl, and tip in any bran left in the sieve/fine-mesh strainer. Add the oats, sugar and baking powder, and mix well.

• Add the nuts and dates to the bowl, and mix well. Put the eggs in a jug/pitcher and add the oil, then mix well. Stir in the banana. Pour this mixture into the flour mixture, and stir to combine – there is no need to beat it. If the mixture seems very stiff, add the milk and stir.

• Divide equally into the muffin cases, and top each one with a pecan. Bake for 20 minutes or until risen and the tops are golden. Remove from the oven and leave on a wire/cooling rack to cool completely.

• You can freeze the muffins for up to 3 months. To take to work the next day, defrost a muffin overnight in a sealed container.

⬛ TIME TO EAT ⬛ These are lovely served warm so, if you can, heat the muffin through on a toaster or in a microwave at work.

← MAKE A CHANGE → For apricot muffins, swap the dates for soft dried apricots. Buy them whole, and chop them up yourself, as the pre-chopped ones tend to be a little dry. Apricots taste great with pecans, but chopped or whole almonds are good too.

Do you usually eat cereal or toast for breakfast? Many of us are in the habit of eating the same thing every day. If you eat fish, eggs and veggies for breakfast now and then, you will be giving your body more variety, and it's no more effort than making porridge. Paleo is about eating simple 'caveman' food, and this breakfast of fish and veggies is packed full of nutrients, without any grains.

PALEO BREAKFAST

1 Little Gem/Bibb lettuce, shredded

1 small avocado, cut in half and pitted

1 tsp olive oil

a squeeze of lemon or lime juice

75g/2½oz cooked salmon flakes or smoked salmon

1 handful of radishes, cut in half

1 tbsp pumpkin seeds

sea salt and freshly ground black pepper

MAKES 1 BREAKFAST

- Put the lettuce in a sealable container. Scoop out the avocado, using a teaspoon, and put on top of the lettuce. Drizzle over the oil, and squeeze over some lemon or lime.

- Add the salmon, radishes and pumpkin seeds, and squeeze over a little more lemon or lime. Season with salt and plenty of pepper. Put the lid on your container and take it to work.

← MAKE A CHANGE → Crayfish, prawns/shrimp and crab all work well instead of salmon, and it's good to vary what you eat.

★ PACKED WITH . . .

Peppery and satisfyingly crunchy, radishes are members of the cruciferous family along with cabbage and broccoli, meaning they help to boost detoxification and support your liver. They also contain a good amount of vitamin C.

You can make this protein-packed frittata in less than 10 minutes. Prepare it in the morning, or the night before if you have an early start ahead. Frittatas are an incredibly versatile dish and a great way to use up bits and pieces from your fridge. Other ingredients that work well include smoked salmon, cooked chicken, pepper/bell pepper, mushroom, spring onion/scallion and courgette/zucchini.

PALEO FRITTATA

- Preheat the grill/broiler. Put the eggs in a bowl with the almond milk and beat lightly, then add plenty of black pepper.

- Warm the oil in an ovenproof frying pan over a medium heat and pour in the egg mixture. Scatter the spinach, ham, parsley and tomatoes over the egg.

- Cook for 3 minutes without stirring, then put the pan under the grill/broiler for 1–2 minutes until the top is golden brown.

- Slide the frittata onto a chopping board. Allow to cool a little and then cut the frittata in half. Wrap both pieces in foil. Take one portion to work, and put the other portion in the fridge – it will keep for breakfast the next day. Eat at room temperature.

4 eggs

1 tbsp unsweetened almond milk

1 tsp extra virgin coconut oil

1 handful of spinach, roughly chopped

25g/1oz ham, roughly chopped

1 tsp finely chopped parsley

4 cherry tomatoes, cut in half

freshly ground black pepper

MAKES 2 BREAKFASTS

★ PACKED WITH . . .

Eggs are an incredibly nutritious and versatile food, packed with healthy fats, protein, vitamins and minerals. Start your day with an egg-based meal and you'll be far more satisfied than with a carb-rich breakfast. As well as B vitamins, zinc and iron, eggs are also a fabulous source of phospholipids; fats which form a vital part of cell membranes and keep our brains in tip-top condition.

2. SALADS AND SLAWS

Grilling/broiling gives chicken a lovely flavour and texture, and this marinade works quickly to add plenty of zing. Make these juicy skewers the night before and in the morning, pop in your lunchbox with whatever salad bits you may have.

CHICKEN AND COURGETTE SALAD

200g/7oz chicken thighs or breast fillets, cut into chunks

1 tbsp olive oil

zest and juice of 1 lime

½ teaspoon frozen chopped ginger or 5mm/¼in piece of root ginger, peeled and grated

1 medium courgette/ zucchini, thickly sliced

1 large handful of salad leaves

freshly ground black pepper

lime wedge, to serve

a chunk of bread, to serve

MAKES 2 LUNCHES

- Put the chicken, oil, lime zest and juice, and ginger in a bowl and mix well.

- Preheat the grill/broiler. Thread the chicken and courgette/zucchini onto two metal skewers (metal conducts heat to the centre of the chicken quicker than wooden skewers). Season with plenty of black pepper.

- Line the grill/broiling pan with foil and put the skewers on top. Cook for 3 minutes, then turn the skewers and cook for a further 3–5 minutes until cooked through.

- Push the chicken and courgette/zucchini off the skewers into a sealable container, ready to take to work. Add the salad leaves and pack a wedge of lime to squeeze over for a zesty dressing, and a chunk of bread to eat alongside.

 **TIP** Pesto makes an instant marinade for chicken. Just mix 1 tsp pesto (see page 151) with 200g/7oz chicken and then grill/broil as above.

★ PACKED WITH . . .

Low in calories and carbohydrates, courgettes/zucchini are also a good source of magnesium and potassium, which help to maintain healthy blood pressure.

This is ideal for pulling together on a Monday morning when you have some leftover roast chicken from Sunday lunch. Spinach, rocket/arugula and red peppers last for ages in the fridge, and, with cooked lentils, make this salad quick and easy to prepare. If you have some leftover cooked veggies from lunch, such as broccoli and carrots, chop them up and pop them in this salad too.

MONDAY MORNING CHICKEN SALAD

1 tbsp rapeseed/canola oil

1 tsp frozen chopped ginger

1 tsp chilli powder

¼ red pepper/bell pepper, deseeded and chopped

75g/2½oz cooked chicken, shredded

50g/1¾oz/¼ cup cooked green lentils, drained (15g/½oz/1½ tbsp dried weight)

a squeeze of lemon juice

1 handful of baby spinach or rocket/arugula leaves

sea salt and freshly ground black pepper

MAKES 1 LUNCH

- Heat the oil in a saucepan over a medium heat and add the ginger and chilli powder. Stir well and cook for 1 minute until the frozen ginger has melted.

- Add the red pepper/bell pepper, chicken and lentils, and stir well. Squeeze over the lemon juice and cook for 2 minutes to help the flavours combine. Season with salt and plenty of pepper.

- Put the spinach leaves in the bottom of your sealable container, then tip the chicken and lentil mixture on top. Put the lid on. The heat will wilt the spinach a little while it cools. Keep cold until you are ready to eat.

TIP Frozen ginger is so useful; just a teaspoonful adds spicy fire to this salad. It's much better value than fresh, as you don't waste any. You can also peel root ginger and freeze it, then grate it from frozen.

★ PACKED WITH . . .

Eating chicken might help to improve your mood. It contains the amino acid tryptophan, which the body converts into the 'happy hormone' serotonin, which helps us to feel relaxed. Chicken is also rich in zinc, which can be low in people who have depression. It might just help with any Monday blues.

This recipe is based on the classic Waldorf salad from New York City; it's packed with nutritious ingredients that you can throw together in the morning. Cox apples are great for this salad, as they have lots of proper apple flavour and they last for ages in the fruit bowl. Hazelnuts are lovely instead of walnuts, if you have those in the cupboard instead.

TURKEY, APPLE AND WALNUT SALAD

1 small red or green eating apple, cored and thinly sliced

a squeeze of lemon juice

75g/2½oz cooked turkey, shredded or sliced

1 celery stalk, chopped, plus the leaves

25g/1oz/scant ¼ cup walnuts, broken into pieces

1 tsp pumpkin seeds

1 tsp Greek or plain yogurt

½ tsp medium curry powder or garam masala

a few radicchio leaves, chopped

MAKES 1 LUNCH

- Put the apple slices in a bowl and squeeze the lemon over, to help prevent browning.
- Add the turkey, celery (not the leaves), walnuts and pumpkin seeds, and stir well.
- In a separate bowl, mix together the yogurt and curry powder. Spoon this into the turkey mixture, and mix to coat all the ingredients.
- Put the radicchio leaves in a sealable container and pile the turkey salad on top. Add the celery leaves. Keep cold until you are ready to eat.

TIP If you buy cooked turkey, read the label to check that it hasn't been coated in weird ingredients and sugar. If you prefer, buy turkey breast fillets and either fry in a non-stick pan for 8 minutes or until cooked through, or roast in the oven alongside your dinner the night before. Cooked turkey will last for 3 days in the fridge.

★ PACKED WITH . . .

Walnuts contain significantly more brain and heart-friendly omega-3 fats than any other nut, making them a great choice for non-fish eaters.

This salad takes just 10 minutes in the morning to pull together, and you will have a warm, satisfying meal to eat at lunchtime. Just a small amount of chorizo gives you loads of flavour.

WARM CHORIZO, TOMATO AND CHICKPEA SALAD

3 small (about 50g/1¾oz) chorizo sausages, roughly sliced

2 spring onions/scallions, diagonally sliced

½ red pepper/bell pepper, deseeded and sliced

1 handful of baby plum or cherry tomatoes, cut in half

50g/1¾oz/heaped ⅓ cup cooked chickpeas, rinsed

1 large handful of rocket/ arugula leaves

freshly ground black pepper

wedge of lemon, to serve (optional)

MAKES 1 LUNCH

• Heat a non-stick frying pan and add the chorizo, spring onions/scallions and red pepper/bell pepper. There is no need to add oil, as the chorizo will release oil as it cooks. Cook for 8 minutes, stirring often, until the chorizo is cooked and has slightly charred edges.

• Add the tomatoes and chickpeas, and stir through. Add plenty of black pepper.

• Tip the mixture into a vacuum food flask, add the rocket/ arugula leaves and seal. Pack the lemon to take with you, if using.

TIME TO EAT Squeeze the lemon over the salad before eating. The rocket/arugula leaves will have wilted slightly in the heat, and the chorizo and peppers should still be warm.

TIP If you can find them, try using brown chickpeas (kala chana) for this salad – they are smaller and nuttier than regular chickpeas.

★ PACKED WITH . . .

Chickpeas are little powerhouses of goodness. As well as iron and bone-friendly manganese, they also contain phytoestrogens that help to maintain healthy hormone balance.

DRESSING UP

A well-made dressing turns a simple salad into something special and brings along its own health benefits. Shop-bought dressings are often disappointing, and they can contain some very weird ingredients, but it's really easy to make your own from scratch. Homemade dressings keep well in the fridge – so get creative and whizz up a couple of jarfuls.

 SOME OF OUR FAVOURITES

EACH MAKES DRESSING

Here are some of the combinations we use all the time. You can happily increase the quantities of any dressing and store it in the fridge for up to 1 week.

CLASSIC DRESSING

This works well with dark green leaves, roasted vegetables and cheese-based salads.

Put **1 tbsp extra virgin olive oil** in a small screwtop jar and add **1 tsp balsamic vinegar** and **1 tsp Dijon mustard**. Shake well. Season with sea salt and freshly ground black pepper.

CREAMY DRESSING

Serve with chicken salads and crunchy leaves, such as cabbage or Little Gem/Bibb lettuce.

Put **1 tbsp plain yogurt** in a small screwtop jar and add **1 tsp extra virgin olive oil**, **1 tsp wholegrain mustard** and **1 tsp apple cider vinegar**. Shake well. Season with sea salt and freshly ground black pepper.

ASIAN DRESSING

This tastes great with kale and noodle-based salads.

Put **1 tbsp toasted sesame oil** in a small screwtop jar and add **1 tbsp apple cider vinegar**, **1 tsp tahini**, **1 tsp tamari (or light soy sauce)** and a **squeeze of lime juice**. Shake well. Season with plenty of freshly ground black pepper.

Most dressings are a simple combination of three or four ingredients: an oil (or other fat), an acid and some flavouring. Here are some ingredients to try:

OILS (OR FAT):

- Extra virgin olive oil – it's great for your heart and a perfect base for a salad dressing
- Flaxseed oil – an excellent source of omega-3 fats and phytoestrogens, which help to keep your hormones in balance
- Toasted sesame oil adds a nutty, slightly Asian flavour to your salad
- Walnut oil – a source of the antioxidant ellagic acid, known for its anti-cancer properties
- Yogurt – if you want a creamy dressing, Greek or plain yogurt is a healthy alternative to mayonnaise
- Tahini or cashew nut butter are dairy-free options if you want a creamier dressing; mix with some olive oil to loosen the texture

ACIDS:

- Apple cider vinegar – choose raw, unfiltered apple cider vinegar for its lovely tangy flavour and health-promoting bacteria
- Balsamic vinegar – choose a good-quality balsamic, because cheaper brands might contain sugar and other unnecessary additives
- Lemon or lime juice adds a zesty taste with a dose of vitamin C, which helps to absorb the iron from your leafy greens
- Red wine vinegar, made from fermented red wine, is a good source of the heart-friendly antioxidant resveratrol

TIP Combine intensely flavoured oils, such as walnut, sesame and flaxseed, with olive oil so that you don't overpower the flavours in your salad.

FLAVOURS:

- Anchovies
- Black pepper
- Capers
- Ginger
- Fresh herbs, such as basil, mint, parsley, coriander/cilantro, chives and garlic
- Lemon, lime or orange zest
- Mustard, such as Dijon or wholegrain
- Sea salt
- Shallots
- Toasted sesame seeds
- Miso – made from fermented soybeans – is a good source of protein and has a host of health benefits. Brown rice miso has a rich savoury flavour, while white rice miso has a lighter, sweeter taste
- Tamari – a wheat-free fermented soy sauce, which is rich in mood-enhancing tryptophan

Hot, peppery watercress and radish combine with smoked mackerel to give you loads of flavour in this easy salad. Beetroot/beet adds a bit of sweetness and is a classic Scandinavian combination with mackerel. Serve with a slice of rye bread, if you like.

SMOKED MACKEREL, WATERCRESS AND RADISH SALAD POT

1 smoked mackerel fillet

1 small cooked beetroot/beet, chopped

1 spring onion/scallion, sliced

4 radishes, sliced

1 large handful of watercress

FOR THE DRESSING

1 tbsp plain yogurt

1 tsp horseradish sauce

a squeeze of lemon

freshly ground black pepper

MAKES 1 LUNCH

- Mix together the dressing ingredients. Spoon the dressing into a small sealable jar or pot.

- Remove the skin from the mackerel, then flake the fish into a sealable container.

- Add the beetroot/beet, spring onion/scallion and radishes, and top with the watercress. Seal the container and pack the dressing to take with you.

TIME TO EAT Pour the dressing over the salad and mix well.

★ PACKED WITH . . .

Smoked mackerel and other oily fish are the best sources of omega-3 fats, which are so important for good mood, joints, skin and overall wellbeing. We are advised to eat three portions a week, so you could double up this recipe and store the second pot in the fridge to eat in a day or two.

Tuna packed in olive oil is juicier and more delicious than tuna packed in water; just drain off most of the oil, leaving a little to make a ready-made salad dressing. This recipe is based on the classic Italian salad, but it contains mild-flavoured spring onion/scallion instead of the usual red onion. A few crisp, raw sugar snap peas are included to boost your veggie intake and because they go so well with the juicy tuna and beans.

TUNA, CANNELLINI BEAN AND SUGAR SNAP SALAD

200g/7oz canned tuna in olive oil, drained and flaked

a squeeze of lemon juice

½ × 400g/14oz can cannellini beans, rinsed and drained

2 spring onions/scallions, thinly sliced

1 handful of sugar snap peas, sliced diagonally

1 handful of small vine or cherry tomatoes, cut in half

1 handful of rocket/ arugula leaves

a few mint or basil leaves (optional)

sea salt and freshly ground black pepper

MAKES 1 LUNCH

- Put the tuna into a large sealable jar or pot. Add a squeeze of lemon juice, and season with a little salt and plenty of black pepper.

- Add the cannellini beans, spring onions/scallions, peas, tomatoes and rocket/arugula leaves.

- Tear the mint or basil leaves over the top, if using, and put the lid on.

★ PACKED WITH . . .

Tuna is a rich source of vitamin B3, which supports the nervous system and helps to maintain healthy cholesterol levels.

1   Eat outside as often as possible. Find a park, garden, canal-side or courtyard, even if it takes you 10 minutes to get there. Recycled air, artificial lighting, piped music, noisy people – you need a change from it.

2   Arrange to meet a friend. Organize lunch for the new colleague.

3   Read a book, listen to a new album and catch up on podcasts. Why not sketch, take photos or write if you want to?

4   Go for a long walk around the nearest park or along a canal or river. Go for a 20-minute run so that you have time to shower afterwards.

5   Find a place to stretch your shoulders, arms and neck to relieve tension from working at a desk.

6   Look out for local lunchtime lectures, talks and music concerts. Visit a gallery or nearby museum.

7   Find a lunchtime yoga, Pilates or stretching class, or book a quick head-and-shoulder massage.

8   Try not to check your phone for an hour. Most things can wait. Look around you, think, and meditate if you like.

This is a wonderfully fresh and zingy salad for a warm day. It is low in carbohydrates, so it's a good choice when you want a lighter option, but it still provides a good dose of protein and healthy fats to stop your energy levels from flagging.

PRAWN, PINK GRAPEFRUIT AND CHICORY SALAD POT

½ pink grapefruit

1 small shallot, finely chopped

1 handful of coriander/ cilantro, finely chopped

1 tsp apple cider vinegar

1 tsp extra virgin olive oil

3 chicory/Belgian endive leaves, sliced

75g/2½oz/scant ⅔ cup cooked peeled prawns/ shrimp

1 tbsp walnuts, chopped

1 handful of watercress

sea salt and freshly ground black pepper

MAKES 1 LUNCH

- Use a sharp knife to remove the skin and pith from the grapefruit. Then cut each segment out of the membrane into a bowl, also catching the juice. Put in a large sealable jar or pot.

- Add the shallot, coriander/cilantro, vinegar and oil, and season with salt and pepper. Stir well.

- Add the chicory/Belgian endive, prawns/shrimp, walnuts and watercress. Seal the jar.

TIME TO EAT Tip the sealed jar upside down to allow the dressing to coat the salad.

★ PACKED WITH . . .

As well as containing vitamin C, pink grapefruit is an excellent source of the plant chemical lycopene, known for its cancer-fighting properties. Research suggests a lycopene-rich diet might help to reduce the risk of prostate cancer in men.

Hot and peppery watercress brings even more vitamin C to this salad and, as a member of the cruciferous family, it also boosts liver detoxification.

Assemble this simple, summery lunch in minutes using a few storecupboard and salad staples. The caper dressing complements the salty fish perfectly. You could spoon some of this salad into a warmed wholemeal/whole-wheat pitta or add a hard-boiled egg if you want to up your protein.

SARDINE, TOMATO, OLIVE AND CAPER SALAD

1 tsp extra virgin olive oil

1 tbsp apple cider vinegar

1 tsp capers, drained

1 tbsp finely chopped parsley

135g/4¾oz can of sardines in olive oil, drained and chopped

1 handful of pitted green olives, cut in half

4 sun-dried tomatoes in olive oil, drained and chopped

5cm/2in piece of cucumber, diced

4 cherry tomatoes, cut in half

1 handful of rocket/arugula

sea salt and freshly ground black pepper

MAKES 1 LUNCH

- Put the oil, vinegar, capers and parsley into a large sealable jar or container. Add a pinch of salt and plenty of black pepper.

- Tip in the sardines. Layer the remaining ingredients on top and fill to the brim with rocket/arugula. Seal the jar or container.

TIME TO EAT Tip the sealed jar or container upside down to allow the dressing to coat the salad.

TIP Save time by packing the can of sardines separately. At lunchtime, simply open, drain and add to your salad before tossing everything together with a fork.

★ PACKED WITH . . .

Canned sardines are a great-value way to help you reach your weekly oily fish quota and get a good dose of omega-3 fats. Don't remove the bones – they will have softened in the can and you'll get an extra boost of calcium from eating them.

Simple to throw together, this satisfying salad really delivers on flavour. It lasts for a couple of days in the fridge and travels well, so it's worth making up an extra pot. Save yourself time by using cooked lentils.

BRAIN-BOOSTER SALAD POT

1 egg

50g/1¾oz/⅓ cup canned borlotti beans, rinsed and drained

50g/1¾oz/¼ cup cooked Puy lentils, rinsed and drained

1 small handful of pitted green olives, cut in half

½ red pepper/bell pepper, deseeded and chopped

1 handful of baby spinach leaves

FOR THE DRESSING
1 tbsp extra virgin olive oil

1 tsp apple cider vinegar

1 small shallot, finely chopped

½ tsp Dijon mustard

3 or 4 canned anchovies, to taste, drained and finely chopped

1 tbsp finely chopped flat leaf parsley

freshly ground black pepper

MAKES 1 LUNCH

- Boil the egg for 10 minutes until hard-boiled, and leave to cool. Meanwhile, mix together the dressing ingredients in a screwtop jar and pour into a large sealable jar or pot.

- Mix together the beans, lentils, olives and red pepper/bell pepper and add to the jar.

- Peel the egg, cut it in half and put it on top of the lentil mixture. Add the spinach leaves. Seal the jar.

TIME TO EAT Tip the sealed jar upside down to allow the dressing to coat the salad.

★ PACKED WITH . . .

Anchovies are a good source of omega-3 fats, which boost mood and keep the brain working at optimal levels, so choose this salad when you need to be at the top of your game. Egg yolks are one of the richest sources of choline, a vital component of brain cell membranes. Lentils, beans and all pulses are a low-fat, low-cost and rich source of fibre, protein, vitamins and minerals.

A perfect pear is delicious, although they can be a tricky fruit to love, because they can take ages to ripen and then quickly go soft. An under-ripe pear is perfectly OK for this lunch, however. If you slice it finely in the morning, it will have softened by the time you want to eat it. Humble cress adds lots of peppery flavour and is so cheap to buy and also really easy to grow.

PEAR, HAZELNUT AND GOAT'S CHEESE SALAD

- Put the hazelnuts in a non-stick saucepan over a low heat and toast for 3–4 minutes until they start to turn golden brown, watching carefully. (It's not the end of the world if you don't have time to though.)

- Meanwhile, put the salad leaves and pear slices in a bowl. Add the oil and vinegar, some salt and plenty of pepper. Mix well to coat the leaves and pear.

- Tear the goat's cheese into pieces, then carefully mix it into the salad with the hazelnuts and cress. Add more pepper and salt, if needed. Put the salad in a sealable container and keep cold until you are ready to eat.

GROW-YOUR-OWN CRESS
Relive your primary school days and grow your own cress. Put a thick layer of paper towel or cotton wool in a container, dampen it with water and sprinkle over cress seeds. Put cling film/plastic wrap over the top and leave on a windowsill. All being well, you will have cress to snip in about 7 days!

25g/1oz/scant ¼ cup hazelnuts

1 handful of mixed salad leaves

1 ripe, or nearly ripe, red or green pear, thinly sliced

1 tsp olive oil

1 tsp white wine vinegar or apple cider vinegar

50g/1¾oz soft goat's cheese

1 tbsp cress

sea salt and freshly ground black pepper

MAKES 1 LUNCH

★ PACKED WITH . . .

If you struggle with digestion, pears can be a great addition to your diet as they are high in the soluble fibre pectin, which binds to toxins and other waste products and helps to soothe and cleanse your colon. Don't peel your pear, as the skin is richer in pectin and health-promoting phytonutrients than the flesh.

Cauliflower and chickpeas taste amazing when roasted. Combined with the feta, this salad is a filling meal, and you won't need any bread with it. Add generous handfuls of whatever leaves you have in the fridge – rocket/arugula and mint taste particularly good.

ROASTED CAULIFLOWER, CHICKPEA, FETA AND POMEGRANATE SALAD

1 small cauliflower (about 325g/11½ oz), broken into bite-size florets

½ × 400g/14oz can chickpeas, rinsed and drained

2 tbsp rapeseed/canola oil

1 tsp smoked paprika

1 handful of pomegranate seeds (see Tip)

1 handful of rocket/arugula leaves

1 handful of mint leaves

50g/1¾oz feta cheese, crumbled

a squeeze of lime juice

sea salt and freshly ground black pepper

MAKES 2 LUNCHES

- Preheat the oven to 180°C/350°F/gas 4. Put the cauliflower in a bowl and add the chickpeas.

- In another bowl, mix together the oil and paprika. Spoon this over the cauliflower and chickpeas, and mix well until well coated.

- Tip the mixture into a baking pan and roast for 15 minutes. Remove from the oven and leave to cool for 5 minutes.

- Add the pomegranate seeds and rocket/arugula leaves. Tear the mint leaves over the top. Add the feta cheese and lime juice, and mix everything together gently.

- Season with salt and pepper. Transfer to two lidded containers. Take one to work and keep the other portion in the fridge until tomorrow.

TIP You can buy pomegranate seeds ready-popped from the fruit, saving you a fiddly job. They freeze well, so if a whole pack is too much, keep them in the freezer and just remove a handful whenever you need them. By the time you get to work, the seeds will have defrosted.

★ PACKED WITH . . .

Feta cheese is lower in fat and calories than most cheeses, and its fresh, tangy flavour means that you don't need a lot to get plenty of taste.

Fresh figs are lusciously sweet and have a unique texture. Give them a try when they're available during the hot summer months, and throw together this classic Mediterranean salad in minutes. If you're lucky enough to have an Italian deli in your neighbourhood, you should be able to find reasonably priced fresh figs and pecorino.

FIG, PECORINO AND RED CHICORY SALAD

3 basil leaves, finely chopped

1 tbsp extra virgin olive oil

1 tsp lemon juice

1 tsp clear honey

2–3 fresh figs, to taste, cut into quarters

25g/1oz pecorino cheese

1 tbsp walnuts

6 red chicory/Belgian endive leaves, shredded

1 handful of rocket/ arugula leaves

sea salt and freshly ground black pepper

MAKES 1 LUNCH

• Put the basil, oil, lemon juice and honey into a small sealable container. Season with sea salt and plenty of black pepper. Put on the lid and shake until well mixed.

• Put the figs in a separate sealable container. Use a potato peeler to slice slithers of pecorino over the figs. Scatter over the walnuts, chicory/Belgian endive and rocket/arugula. Seal the container and pack the dressing to take with you.

TIME TO EAT Pour the dressing over the salad and mix thoroughly.

← MAKE A CHANGE → Crumbly goat's cheese or a few slices of Parma ham/prosciutto would also work well in this salad.

★ PACKED WITH . . .

Full of fibre, figs help to regulate your digestive system, as you may already know. They are also a good source of bone-strengthening calcium and potassium to help keep your blood pressure within a healthy range.

PICK 'N' MIX SALADS

There's no reason why you can't throw together a different and delicious salad every day of the week if you stock up on some basics.

You can buy plenty of salads in high-street shops today, but they tend to be mean on the main ingredients, heavy on the stringy salad leaves or bulked out with soggy pasta. By making your own, you can make sure you get enough protein and can miss out on the bits you don't like.

Clever layering will keep your salad fresh and crunchy until lunchtime. Start with a dressing, then layer your ingredients on top, starting with the heavier items at the bottom and finishing with the leafy greens on top. Take your pick from our suggestions and get creative.

DRESSING LAYER:

Pour your dressing into the bottom of the jar or pot (see the dressings on pages 52–3). Tip the sealed jar upside down to allow the dressing to coat the salad just before eating.

ENERGY LAYER:

These are your starchy carbs and should be no more than a quarter of your jar or pot. Choose from:

- Brown or wild rice
- Brown rice noodles
- Cooked lentils
- Chickpeas
- Kidney beans
- Borlotti beans
- Broad/fava beans
- Cannellini beans or black beans
- Quinoa
- Roasted root veggies, such as beetroot/beets, squash, sweet potato
- Wholemeal/whole-wheat pasta

ENDURANCE LAYER:

This is your protein layer, which will help to keep you fuller for longer. This layer should be a quarter of your jar. Choose from:

- Feta or goat's cheese
- Hard-boiled egg
- Nuts or seeds
- Canned tuna, sardines or anchovies
- Smoked fish
- Roasted or poached chicken, turkey or salmon

DELI LAYER:

Add a tablespoonful or two of these ingredients when you're low on fresh veggies:

- Marinated artichokes or peppers/bell peppers
- Sun-dried or sun-blush tomatoes
- Olives

IMMUNE-BOOSTING LAYER:

Pile in these chopped raw salad items to fill at least another quarter of the jar. Try to vary your shopping each week:

- Avocado
- Broccoli florets
- Celery
- Cherry or baby plum tomatoes
- Courgette/zucchini
- Cucumber
- Fennel
- Frozen peas or edamame beans/green soybeans
- Peppers/bell peppers
- Pomegranate seeds
- Radishes
- Seedless grapes
- Spring onions/scallions
- Sugar snap peas

LEAFY-GOODNESS LAYER:

Fill your jar to the brim with super-greens. Tear or chop the leaves so that they fit in. Add herbs, if you have them, for a hit of extra flavour. Choose from:

- Cabbage
- Chicory/Belgian endive
- Kale
- Little Gem/Bibb or romaine lettuce
- Mint or parsley
- Rocket/arugula
- Salad cress
- Spinach or watercress

Spiralizers are now fairly low cost to buy and they can turn a single courgette/zucchini into a bowlful of noodle-length ribbons. You can pull this lunch together in the morning, and just add the avocado when you are ready to eat. If you want to prepare the avocado at home, add it last and squeeze more lemon juice over to help stop any browning.

COURGETTI, PEA AND AVOCADO SALAD POT

1 tbsp olive oil

zest of ½ lemon, and a squeeze of lemon juice

50g/1¾oz/scant ½ cup frozen petits pois

1 courgette/zucchini

1 handful of mint leaves

1 handful of pea shoots

1 tbsp pumpkin seeds

1 ripe avocado

sea salt and freshly ground black pepper

MAKES 1 LUNCH

- Put the oil in a large sealable jar or lidded pot, then add the lemon zest and juice. Add salt and plenty of pepper.

- Tip in the frozen petits pois. Spiralize the courgette/zucchini (or slice) straight into the jar; it takes just a few seconds.

- Tear the mint leaves, and add to the jar with the pea shoots and pumpkin seeds. Seal the jar. Pack the avocado to take with you. The peas will have defrosted by lunchtime.

TIME TO EAT   Tip the sealed jar to allow the dressing to coat the salad. Cut open the avocado, discard the pit, and, using a teaspoon, scoop out chunks on to your salad.

★ PACKED WITH . . .

Peas are a fantastic source of vitamin K, which is important for wound healing and healthy bones – and the healthy fats in the avocado improve absorption of this fat-soluble nutrient.

★ PACKED WITH . . .

Beluga lentils are loaded with anthocyanins – powerful antioxidants, which give the lentils their lustrous black colour. Anthocyanins help to fight off free-radical damage and so may help to protect us from cancer and heart disease as well as keeping wrinkles at bay.

This salad uses delicious storecupboard ingredients, so you can throw it together in the morning. Feta cheese and baby plum tomatoes last for ages in the fridge, so this is a good option for the end of the week. It's worth having a couple of packs of pre-cooked lentils in your cupboard for when time is short. They are packed with protein, and have a rich satisfying taste.

BELUGA LENTILS, ROASTED RED PEPPER AND FETA SALAD

1 small roasted red pepper/
bell pepper, drained and
cut into thick pieces

50g/1¾oz/⅓ cup cooked
Beluga black lentils

1 handful of pitted
Kalamata (purple) olives

1 handful of baby plum
tomatoes, cut in half

1 tsp balsamic vinegar

1 handful of baby spinach
leaves or rocket/arugula

25g/1oz feta cheese,
crumbled

1 tsp pumpkin seeds

freshly ground black pepper

MAKES 1 LUNCH

- Put the pepper into a bowl. Add the lentils, olives, tomatoes and balsamic vinegar, and mix carefully.

- Put the spinach leaves in a sealable container. Put the pepper mixture on top, followed by the feta cheese and pumpkin seeds. Add plenty of pepper (the feta is salty, so there is no need to add any salt).

- Put the lid on the container, and take to work.

ROASTING PEPPERS If you prefer to roast your own peppers/bell peppers, do 3–4 at a time. It is worth doing if you find a bag of bargain peppers, and this way you can make orange, yellow and green roasted peppers, which are not often sold in the shops.

Preheat the oven to 200°C/400°F/gas 6. Cut the peppers into quarters, and deseed them. Put in a roasting pan and drizzle over a little olive oil. Roast for 25 minutes or until the skins start to blacken. Remove from the oven and put in a sealable container. After about 30 minutes the skins will be easy to peel off. You can freeze the peppers, if you like, once completely cool.

You'll feel very virtuous tucking into a bowl of this fantastic salad bursting with fresh, zingy flavours and heaps of nutrients. This salad will keep well in the fridge for a couple of days, so you can easily double the quantity.

KALE, ALMOND, QUINOA AND GOJI BERRY SALAD

60g/2¼oz/⅓ cup quinoa

1 tbsp almonds

1 large handful of curly kale leaves, central stalks removed

1 tsp extra virgin olive oil

a pinch of sea salt

juice of ½ lemon

1 tsp dried goji berries

1 small handful of mint leaves, finely chopped

1 small handful of parsley leaves, finely chopped

MAKES 1 LUNCH

- Put the quinoa in a pan with 125ml/4fl oz/½ cup water, bring to the boil, then cover and simmer until all the water is absorbed and the quinoa is soft and fluffy.

- Put the almonds in a small saucepan and toast them over a medium heat for 1–2 minutes until golden brown, stirring regularly. Remove from the pan and leave to cool.

- Meanwhile, put the kale leaves in a bowl and add the oil, salt and lemon juice, then massage the leaves to make sure that they are well coated. Add the remaining ingredients to the kale and mix together well.

- Transfer to a large sealable jar or container and keep cold until ready to eat.

★ PACKED WITH . . .

Sturdy kale makes a great base for a packed lunch, and even benefits from being left to marinate in a dressing for a few hours, becoming easier to chew and digest. As well as being one of the highest antioxidant foods available, kale is an excellent plant source of easily-absorbed calcium, which is so important for bone health. The quinoa, almonds and goji berries contain protein, so you'll feel nicely satisfied.

High in plant protein and brimming with nutrients, this is definitely a superhero salad that will leave you feeling energized until it's time to go home. If you don't have time to cook rice in the morning, prepare it the night before and chill it in the fridge overnight.

SUPERFOOD SALAD POT WITH SPIRULINA AND NORI FLAKES

2 tbsp wild rice

1 tsp sunflower seeds

1 tsp sesame seeds

1 tsp spirulina flakes (optional)

2 tbsp frozen peas

½ red pepper/bell pepper, deseeded and diced

1 handful of alfalfa sprouts, thoroughly rinsed

1 handful of rocket/ arugula

FOR THE DRESSING
1 tsp tamari or light soy sauce

1 tsp extra virgin olive oil

1 tsp cold-pressed flaxseed oil

1 squeeze of lime juice

1 tbsp nori flakes

freshly ground black pepper

MAKES 1 LUNCH

- Cook the rice in 100ml/3½fl oz/scant ½ cup water for 40 minutes or according to the packet instructions. Drain and leave to cool.

- Put the sunflower seeds and sesame seeds in a small saucepan and toast them over a medium heat for 1–2 minutes until golden brown. Remove from the pan and leave to cool.

- Meanwhile, mix together all the dressing ingredients in a large sealable jar or pot. Add the cooled rice. Add the spirulina flakes (if using), sunflower seeds, sesame seeds, peas, red pepper/bell pepper, alfalfa sprouts and rocket/ arugula and seal the jar.

TIME TO EAT   Tip the sealed jar upside down to allow the dressing to coat the salad.

★ PACKED WITH . . .

Adding spirulina elevates the nutrient levels of this salad from super to out of this world! Spirulina is a freshwater blue–green algae, which is high in iron and protein, and also in vitamin B_{12}, which provides energy and is vital for growth and brain function. Vegetarians often lack vitamin B_{12} in their diet, so it is particularly useful to buy spirulina powder or flakes to add to recipes if you don't eat meat.

Packed with veggies and full of flavour, this crunchy salad will brighten even the toughest of days. You can prepare it the night before, and double the quantities if you like, as it lasts well in the fridge for up to 2 days.

NUTTY NOODLE SALAD

50g/1¾oz brown vermicelli rice noodles

50g/1¾oz/scant ½ cup cashew nuts

juice of ½ lime

1 tbsp tamari or light soy sauce

½ fresh red chilli, deseeded and chopped

1 tsp extra virgin olive oil

1 tsp clear honey

1 tsp tahini

1 tbsp sugar-free peanut butter

1 carrot, peeled

½ red pepper/bell pepper, deseeded and diced

1 spring onion/scallion, sliced

2 tbsp frozen peas

2 Chinese/napa cabbage leaves, shredded

MAKES 1 LUNCH

- Put the noodles in a bowl and pour over boiling water to cover. Leave for 3 minutes, then drain and rinse in cold water. Transfer to a sealable container.

- Meanwhile, toast the cashew nuts by putting them in a non-stick saucepan over a medium heat. Stir for 2 minutes or until the nuts start to turn golden brown. Remove from the pan and set aside.

- Put the lime juice, tamari, chilli, oil, honey, tahini and peanut butter into a small sealable container. Put the lid on and shake well until thoroughly mixed.

- Use a peeler or spiralizer to cut the carrot into ribbons directly on top of the noodles.

- Scatter over the pepper/bell pepper, spring onion/scallion, peas and cabbage. Put the cashews on top. Seal the container and pack the dressing to take with you. The peas will have defrosted by lunchtime.

 TIME TO EAT Pour the dressing over the salad and mix thoroughly.

★ PACKED WITH . . .

Lighter and crunchier than most cabbages, Chinese/napa cabbage is rich in detoxifying sulfur, which helps to keep your skin, nails and hair strong and healthy.

This is a stir-fry salad that you can make the night before, if you like. The broccoli, cashew nuts, lemon and chilli are a classic Chinese combination and go so well together. Quinoa cooks quicker than rice and also contains protein. If you have some leftover rice, you could use that instead, and just stir it in after the broccoli has cooked.

BROCCOLI, CASHEW AND QUINOA SALAD

2 tbsp red quinoa

1 tsp rapeseed/canola oil

½ tsp chilli powder

25g/1oz/¼ cup frozen edamame beans/green soybeans or peas

100g/3½oz purple sprouting broccoli, cut into bite-size pieces

50g/1¾oz/scant ½ cup cashew nuts

1 tbsp tamari or light soy sauce

a squeeze of lemon

freshly ground black pepper

MAKES 1 LUNCH

- Put the quinoa in a non-stick saucepan with 100ml/ 3½fl oz/scant ½ cup boiling water. Bring to the boil, then reduce the heat and simmer over a low heat for 10 minutes or until the water is absorbed, then stir well, and leave to one side to cool a little.

- Meanwhile, heat the oil in a non-stick frying pan and add the chilli powder, edamame/green soybeans and broccoli. Add 1 tablespoon boiling water. Stir well, cover and cook over a medium heat for 5 minutes, stirring occasionally, until the broccoli has softened slightly.

- Add the cashew nuts and tamari, and stir well. Cook for a further 2 minutes, uncovered, stirring to mix well.

- Transfer the broccoli and cashew mixture to the quinoa and mix well to combine. Add the lemon juice and plenty of black pepper. Transfer to a sealable container, put the lid on and take to work.

★ PACKED WITH . . .

Rich in antioxidants, broccoli also contains the powerful detoxifier indole-3-carbinol (I3C). I3C is particularly helpful in ridding the body of excess oestrogen and could potentially protect against breast cancer.

Black rice makes a nutritious change from white rice. Perhaps surprisingly, black rice is an even richer source of anthocyanins than blackberries and blueberries, which are known as good sources. You can buy pouches of ready-cooked black rice to keep in the cupboard to pull together this quick, Mexican-inspired lunch.

SPEEDY BURRITO BOWL

75g/2½oz/½ cup canned kidney beans, drained and rinsed

½ spring onion/scallion, sliced

¼ red pepper/bell pepper, deseeded and chopped

½ avocado, flesh chopped

1 handful of cherry or baby plum tomatoes, cut into quarters

½ tsp mild chilli powder

1 tsp olive oil

1 handful of coriander/cilantro leaves, chopped (optional)

75g/2½oz/scant ½ cup cooked black rice

a squeeze of lime

sea salt and freshly ground black pepper

MAKES 1 LUNCH

- Put the kidney beans, spring onion/scallion, red pepper/bell pepper, avocado and tomatoes in a bowl.
- In a separate bowl, mix together the chilli powder, olive oil and coriander/cilantro, if using, and stir. Pour into the kidney bean mixture and stir well. Add sea salt to taste.
- Put the cooked rice at one end of a sealable container and season with salt and pepper. Put the kidney bean mixture alongside and squeeze over the lime. Put the lid on and keep cold until you are ready to eat.

★ PACKED WITH . . .

Avocados are amazingly healthy. They are packed with heart-friendly monounsaturated fat, vitamin E, folic acid, vitamin B₃ and potassium.

SLAWS

Grate up some veggies for a delicious, healthy slaw. Far more interesting than a few chopped-up carrot sticks, a slaw is an easy way to get your seven-a-day. Add a large spoonful to a sandwich or just take a pot to work to eat whenever you feel in need of a nutrient boost. Make a bowlful at the start of the week and you can add nuts, fish, turkey or cheese on day two and three to make things more interesting.

Shop-bought slaws contain far more mayo, sugar and preservatives than any of us need or really want. You don't even need mayo; yogurt and nut milks also make good, creamy dressings, and you only need a small amount to bring your slaw together. You can skip these altogether and just use a salad dressing (see pages 52–53) or a simple mix of white wine vinegar and lemon or lime juice.

CELERIAC SLAW

Celeriac is very easy to grate, so here is a quick way to get this under-used vegetable into your diet. You will see pots of celeriac salads in French delis, where it is used alongside smoked fish and meats and in sandwiches. It has a lovely mild, celery flavour.

MAKES LUNCHES

Cut the outside off **100g/3½oz celeriac** using a sharp knife. Grate the celeriac using a box grater and tip it into a bowl. Add **1 tbsp Greek yogurt**, the **zest and juice of 1 lime** and **1 tsp black sesame seeds**. Tear or chop **1 handful of dill, mint or parsley leaves** and add to the bowl. Mix well. Season with salt and freshly ground black pepper. Put into a sealable container. Keep cold until you are ready to eat. The slaw will keep for 3 days, sealed, in the fridge.

VEGGIES:

Grate, slice or spiralize a variety of veggies to make the base for your slaw.

- Cabbage
- Carrots
- Celeriac
- Celery
- Courgette/zucchini
- Edamame beans/green soybeans
- Fennel
- Peas
- Radishes
- Beetroot/beets
- Red onion
- Spring onion/scallion

FRUITS:

Fresh and dried fruits work well in slaws, and just a little goes a long way, adding a hit of sweetness and extra fibre.

- Apple
- Dried apricots
- Grapefruit
- Orange
- Parsley
- Pear
- Pomegranate
- Sultanas/golden raisins
- Sunflower seeds

FRESH HERBS:

If you have some fresh herbs, great, add a handful.

- Chives
- Coriander/cilantro
- Dill
- Mint

SEEDS:

Seeds add crunch, flavour and nutrients, and makes your slaw more interesting than any you can buy.

- Fennel seeds
- Pumpkin seeds
- Sesame seeds

SUMMER VEGETABLE SLAW

A couple of minutes of grating and chopping and you have a generous bowlful of delicious, juicy veggies that only need a light citrus dressing. It is lovely in a sandwich on its own, with hummus in a pitta bread, or with roasted salmon on top.

MAKES 1 LUNCH

Grate **1 carrot** and **1 small courgette/zucchini**, then tip them into a bowl. Add **2 sliced spring onions/scallions, 3 sliced or chopped radishes, 1 tbsp pumpkin seeds** and **1 handful of mint leaves**. Put **1 tsp extra virgin olive oil** in a small bowl and add a **squeeze of lime juice** (or **1 tsp white wine vinegar**). Season with salt and freshly ground black pepper, and mix well. Pour the dressing over the vegetables and mix to combine. Transfer to a sealable container. Keep cold until you are ready to eat.

3. FILLING FLASKS

You only need a small amount of chorizo to add lots of flavour to this soup. Ready-to-eat cured chorizo lasts for a couple of weeks in the fridge, so it's a great ingredient to have on standby. Choose the best-quality chorizo you can find, which should be lower in fat and free from artificial preservatives.

BLACK BEAN AND CHORIZO SOUP

1 tbsp rapeseed/canola oil

125g/4½oz chorizo, chopped

1 small red onion, thinly sliced

2 tsp frozen chopped garlic or 2 garlic cloves, chopped

2 celery stalks, thinly sliced

1 Romano red pepper, deseeded and thinly sliced

1 tsp smoked paprika, plus extra, if needed

400g/14oz can black beans, rinsed and drained

400g/14oz passata or chopped tomatoes

sea salt and freshly ground black pepper

lime wedge (optional)

MAKES 4 LUNCHES

- Heat the oil in a large saucepan, then add the chorizo, red onion, garlic, celery and Romano pepper. Stir well and cook for 5 minutes until the chorizo starts to release its oil.

- Add the paprika and stir well. Add the black beans, passata and 300ml/10½fl oz/1¼ cups water, and stir well. Bring to the boil, then reduce the heat and simmer for 20 minutes or until the soup is thickened.

- Season with salt and pepper, and a little more paprika, if you like.

- Divide the soup among four freezerproof containers, and freeze for up to 3 months any that you don't want to eat soon. Reheat a portion before you go to work and transfer to a vacuum food flask – or reheat it at work. Pack the lime to take with you, if using.

TIME TO EAT Reheat at work, if necessary, and squeeze over some lime before eating.

TIP To save time, we use cured chorizo, rather than raw, cooking chorizo. Buy the whole sausage rings rather than ready chopped; ready chopped pieces can be a little dry.

★ PACKED WITH . . .

Combining chorizo with black beans will provide you with a good dose of vitamin B_1, which helps turn food into energy.

You can make this spicy, warming soup before you go to work – it is so quick and easy. Tom yum paste adds a delicious flavour to the prawns/shrimp and udon noodles. The soup has plenty of vegetables in it too, so it is a well-balanced lunch in a bowl.

PRAWN TOM YUM SOUP

- Put the kettle on and pour 500ml/17fl oz/2 cups boiling water into a saucepan. Add the tom yum paste and stir for a few seconds until it dissolves.

- Add the prawns/shrimp, green beans, spring onions/scallions, mushrooms, noodles and pepper/bell pepper.

- Bring to the boil, then simmer for 10 minutes. Season with a little black pepper.

- Pour one portion into a vacuum food flask to take to work. The second portion will keep well in the fridge until tomorrow.

 **TIP** Tom yum soup is from Thailand, and shop-bought pastes contain Thai herbs such as kaffir lime leaves, galangal and lemongrass. No one wants to chop these before work, and a paste works really well. A jar of paste lasts only a week or so in the fridge, so spoon it into an ice-cube tray and freeze. Just add to boiling water whenever you want to make this soup.

1 heaped tbsp tom yum paste (see Tip)

125g/4½oz/1 cup frozen cooked peeled king prawns/jumbo shrimp

50g/1¾oz/⅓ cup fine green beans, cut into 1cm/½in pieces

2 spring onions/scallions, diagonally sliced

4 mushrooms, peeled and thinly sliced

50g/1¾oz dried brown rice udon noodles

¼ red pepper/bell pepper, deseeded and thinly sliced

freshly ground black pepper

MAKES 2 LUNCHES

★ PACKED WITH . . .

Galangal is a main ingredient in tom yum paste. It's a member of the ginger family with anti-inflammatory effects and has traditionally been used to combat nausea.

SOUP TOPPERS AND STIR-INS

Who said soup had to be boring? Give your soup a boost of flavour and extra nutrients with a topper or stir-in. If you have made a batch of soup to last a few lunches, this is a simple way to add variety.

SPRINKLE POT

Liven up your soup with this fragrant mix. It works well with the Prawn Tom Yum Soup (see page 95).

MAKES 1 TOPPING

Put **1 finely chopped spring onion/scallion** in a small sealable container. Peel and grate **5mm/¼in root ginger**, and deseed and finely chop **¼ red chilli**. Add both to the container. Keep cold until ready to eat, then sprinkle the mix over your hot soup.

TIP

Small jam/jelly jars, like the ones you find in hotels, are perfect containers to carry your soup toppers to work.

SPICY ROASTED SEED MIX

Add a bit of crunch to soups with this punchy mix. This makes the perfect topping for Up-beet Soup (see page 105).

MAKES 5 TOPPINGS

Preheat the oven to 200°C/400°F/gas 6. Put **2 tbsp pumpkin seeds** in a bowl and add **2 tbsp sunflower seeds** and **1 tbsp sesame seeds**. Add **1 tsp rapeseed/canola oil**, **½ tsp chilli powder** and **1 tbsp tamari (or light soy sauce)**. Mix well. Spread the seeds evenly over a baking sheet and roast for 3 minutes, then give the mixture a good stir. Cook for another 3 minutes or until the pumpkin seeds start to pop. Remove from the oven and leave to cool. Store in an airtight container in the fridge for up to 2 weeks. Put 1 tablespoonful in a small sealable container to take to work and sprinkle it over your hot soup.

TOASTED NUTS

Toasting brings out the flavour of nuts and makes them extra crunchy. Use cashew nuts, hazelnuts, pistachio nuts, pecan nuts or almonds, either on their own or as a mixture.

MAKES 5 TOPPINGS

Put **5 tbsp of nuts** in a non-stick frying pan and cook over a medium heat for 2–5 minutes, checking carefully, until they are golden brown. Toss the nuts frequently so that they toast evenly and don't burn. Remove from the pan to cool. Store in an airtight container in the fridge for up to 2 weeks. Put 1 tablespoonful in a small sealable container to take to work, and sprinkle it over your hot soup.

SOUPER GREENS STIR-IN

It takes seconds to whizz this up using a hand-held blender. Use whatever green leaves need eating up. Try it in the Immune-boosting Soup (see page 106).

MAKES 1 TOPPING

Put **2 large handfuls of spinach (or watercress, rocket/arugula or kale)** into a blender or food processor. Add **2 tbsp parsley (or coriander/cilantro or basil leaves)**, a **squeeze of lemon juice**, **1 tsp extra virgin olive oil** and **1 chopped garlic clove** (optional). Season with freshly ground black pepper, and whizz for a few seconds. Taste and add more black pepper if needed. Transfer to a sealed container to take to work. Keep cold until you are ready to eat.

PARMESAN CROUTONS

Here is a good way to get a bread fix without eating that much bread. Leftover, going-stale bread is perfect for making croûtons, and, mixed with a little Parmesan, is delicious. Please don't buy mass-produced croûtons – they are so oily and can be months old. You can add croûtons to any soup, and can also sprinkle them over salads.

MAKES 5 TOPPINGS

Preheat the oven to 200°C/400°F/gas 6. Tear **100g/3½oz slightly stale rye sourdough bread** (or whatever you have) into bite-size chunks into a bowl. Add **1 tbsp olive oil** and **1 tbsp grated Parmesan cheese**. Use your hands to mix really well. Spread evenly onto a baking sheet and put in the oven for 10–15 minutes, shaking the baking sheet every minute or so, until the croûtons are golden and crispy. Remove from the oven and leave to cool. Store in an airtight container for up to 5 days. Put 1 tablespoonful in a small sealable container to take to work, and sprinkle it over your hot soup.

Perfect for any day when you know you will need something warming and nutritious to eat at lunchtime. Kids love this too, so it's a great meal for a packed school lunch in a food flask. Serve with crusty bread to dip in. The butter beans are a good source of protein, making this surprisingly filling.

TOMATO <u>AND</u> BUTTER BEAN SOUP

1 tbsp rapeseed/canola oil

1 small red onion, chopped

1 celery stalk, sliced

1 carrot, chopped

1 tsp frozen chopped garlic or 1 garlic clove, chopped (see Tip)

400g/14oz can chopped tomatoes

400g/14oz can butter beans, rinsed and drained

sea salt and freshly ground black pepper

MAKES 4 LUNCHES

- Heat the oil in a large saucepan. Add the onion, celery, carrot and garlic. Cover and cook for 10 minutes until softened.

- Add the tomatoes and butter beans, and 200ml/7fl oz/ scant 1 cup boiling water. Stir well, and bring back to the boil, then reduce the heat and simmer for 10 minutes.

- Whizz the soup using a blender or food processor until smooth. Season with salt and plenty of black pepper.

- Divide the soup among four freezerproof containers, then cool and freeze for up to 3 months any that you don't want to eat soon. Defrost overnight in the fridge. Reheat a portion before you go to work and transfer to a vacuum food flask – or reheat it at work.

≋ TIP ≋ Frozen garlic is brilliant for busy people. Save fresh garlic for when you want to use whole cloves, and use frozen ready-chopped garlic for soups and stews. It's great value, and you won't be wasting food. One teaspoon of frozen garlic equals about one garlic clove.

★ PACKED WITH . . .

Heating tomatoes aids the release of their protective carotenoids, which help to guard against certain cancers and sun damage. The oil used in the soup helps to aid absorption of these fat-soluble nutrients.

Beautifully pale yellow and mildly spiced, this aromatic soup brings the humble cauliflower to life. The almonds make the soup creamy and sustaining. Eat it with a wholemeal chapati, if you like. The soup is lovely with a little yogurt stirred in, so take a small pot with you to work, and eat the rest mid-afternoon with some fruit or nuts.

SPICY CAULIFLOWER AND ALMOND SOUP

- 1 tbsp coconut or rapeseed/canola oil

- 1 large onion, chopped

- 2 tsp frozen chopped garlic or 2 garlic cloves, chopped

- 2 tsp mild curry powder

- 1 large cauliflower, chopped

- 1l/35fl oz/4⅓ cups vegetable stock

- 2 tbsp ground almonds

- sea salt and freshly ground black pepper

- 2 tbsp plain or coconut yogurt, to serve

MAKES 4 LUNCHES

- Heat the oil in a large saucepan over a medium heat and add the onion and garlic. Cook for 5 minutes until softened.

- Add the curry powder and cauliflower. Stir well until the cauliflower is well coated in the spices.

- Pour in the vegetable stock, bring to the boil, then reduce the heat and simmer for 10 minutes or until the cauliflower is tender. Stir in the ground almonds.

- Transfer the mixture to a blender or food processor and whizz until smooth. Season with salt and plenty of black pepper.

- Divide the soup among four freezerproof containers, then cool and freeze for up to 3 months any that you don't want to eat soon. Defrost overnight in the fridge. Reheat a portion before you go to work and transfer to a vacuum food flask – or reheat it at work. Pack the yogurt to take with you.

 TIME TO EAT Reheat at work, if necessary, and add a swirl of yogurt before eating.

★ PACKED WITH . . .

As part of the cruciferous vegetable family (along with broccoli, Brussels sprouts and cabbage), cauliflower is rich in disease-fighting sulfurane.

If you're a fan of traditional leek and potato soup, you'll love this more sustaining combination. Butter beans not only make a creamy soup, but they also give you extra fibre and nutrients to keep you energized through a long afternoon.

LEEK, BUTTER BEAN AND ROSEMARY SOUP

- Heat the oil in a large saucepan over a medium heat, and add the onion. Cook for 5 minutes or until the onion is softened.

- Add the rosemary, leeks and garlic, and cook for 2 minutes, then add the butter beans and stock. Bring to the boil, then reduce the heat and simmer for 5 minutes.

- Put all the ingredients into a blender or food processor and whizz until smooth. Season with salt and plenty of black pepper.

- Divide the soup among four freezerproof containers, then cool and freeze for up to 3 months any that you don't want to eat soon. Defrost overnight in the fridge. Reheat a portion before you go to work and transfer to a vacuum food flask – or reheat it at work. Pack the sunflower seeds to take with you.

 TIME TO EAT Reheat at work, if necessary, and sprinkle with seeds before eating.

1 tbsp rapeseed/canola oil

1 onion, chopped

2 tsp finely chopped rosemary

5 leeks, sliced

3 tsp frozen chopped garlic or 3 garlic cloves, chopped

400g/14oz can butter beans, rinsed and drained

1l/35fl oz/4⅓ cups vegetable stock

sea salt and freshly ground black pepper

1 tsp sunflower or pumpkin seeds, to serve

MAKES 4 LUNCHES

★ PACKED WITH . . .

Leek, onion and garlic all come from the allium family. They are prized for their strong, punchy flavours, heart-protective properties and their ability to ease the symptoms of colds and flu.

 TIP Rosemary is so easy to grow, surviving lack of watering, so it's well worth growing a pot on a windowsill.

★ PACKED WITH ...

Beetroot/beet is crammed with iron, calcium, folate, betaine, B vitamins and antioxidants, which combine to make it a great detoxifier. A shorter cooking time means you'll get the most from all these nutrients.

This crimson soup looks and tastes amazing. Even if you think you are not a fan of beetroot/beet, give it a go; it's delicious combined with lemon and spices. Instead of using fresh, you could use vacuum-packed pre-cooked beetroot/beets to save time. Cook the soup for just 5 minutes before blending. Take a small pot of plain yogurt with you to work, and stir a spoonful into the soup when you are ready to eat. Finish the pot mid-afternoon with some fruit or nuts.

UP-BEET SOUP

1 tbsp rapeseed/canola oil

1 large red onion, chopped

2 tsp frozen chopped garlic or 2 garlic cloves, chopped

3 celery stalks, sliced

1 tsp ground cumin

1 tsp ground coriander

1 tsp dried chilli/hot pepper flakes

500g/1lb 2oz beetroot/beet, roughly chopped

2 tbsp ground almonds

juice of 1 lemon

sea salt and freshly ground black pepper

plain yogurt, to serve

MAKES 4 LUNCHES

- Heat the oil in a large saucepan over a medium heat. Add the onion, garlic and celery, and cook for 5 minutes or until softened.

- Add the cumin, coriander and chilli, then add the beetroot/beet and pour in 1.50l/52fl oz/6½ cups water. Bring to the boil, then reduce the heat and simmer for 10 minutes or until the beetroot is just tender.

- Transfer the mixture to a blender or food processor and whizz until smooth. Add the ground almonds and whizz again.

Add the lemon juice and season with salt and plenty of pepper.

- Divide the soup among four freezerproof containers and freeze for up to 3 months any that you don't want to eat soon. Defrost overnight in the fridge. Reheat a portion before you go to work and transfer to a vacuum food flask – or reheat it at work. Pack the yogurt to take with you.

TIME TO EAT Reheat at work, if necessary, and add a swirl of yogurt before eating.

TIP Ground almonds are packed with protein, and just a little adds a lovely richness to soups, stews and curries.

If you're feeling sniffly or simply in need of a warming bowl of deliciousness on a chilly day, then pack yourself a large serving of this fiery, orange soup, filled with an army of cold-busting ingredients. The soup is delicious with a sprinkle of pumpkin seeds on top, so it's worth packing some in your lunchbox. If you're short of time there's no need to blend this soup – just keep it chunky.

IMMUNE-BOOSTING SOUP

1 tbsp coconut or rapeseed/canola oil

2 tsp frozen chopped garlic or 2 garlic cloves, chopped

1 tsp frozen chopped ginger or 2.5cm/1in piece of root ginger, peeled and grated

400g/14oz pumpkin or butternut squash, peeled, deseeded and cut into cubes

1 red onion, finely chopped

1 tbsp ground turmeric

½ tsp ground cayenne pepper

1.50l/52fl oz/6½ cups vegetable stock

100g/3½oz/heaped ½ cup dried red lentils

1 yellow or orange pepper/bell pepper, deseeded and chopped

1 red chilli, deseeded and finely chopped

400ml/14fl oz/1¾ cups canned coconut milk

sea salt and freshly ground black pepper

pumpkin seeds, for sprinkling (optional)

MAKES 4 LUNCHES

• Heat the oil over a medium heat, then add the garlic, ginger, pumpkin and onion. Stir well and cook for 5 minutes or until the onion is softened.

• Add the turmeric and cayenne pepper. Stir well then pour in the stock and lentils.

• Bring to the boil, then reduce the heat and simmer for 10 minutes.

• Remove from the heat, add the pepper and chilli, and stir in the milk.

• Pour the mixture into a blender or food processor and whizz until smooth. Season with salt and plenty of black pepper.

• Divide the soup among four freezerproof containers, and freeze for up to 3 months any that you don't want to eat soon. Defrost overnight in the fridge. Reheat a portion before you go to work and transfer to a vacuum food flask – or reheat it at work. Pack the pumpkin seeds to take with you, if using.

▰ TIME TO EAT ▰ Reheat at work, if necessary, and sprinkle with pumpkin seeds before eating.

★ PACKED WITH . . .

Turmeric, the bright yellow spice commonly used in Indian cookery, contains the potent compound curcumin, which has powerful anti-inflammatory properties. If you can find the fresh root, that's even better: use 1cm/½in, peeled and grated.

You can rustle up this earthy soup from start to finish in under 30 minutes. Aim to use at least two mushroom varieties to achieve depth of flavour. Serve with a seeded bread roll or bagel for a filling lunch.

CREAMY WILD MUSHROOM SOUP

1 tbsp rapeseed/canola oil

1 handful of shallots, finely chopped

2 tsp frozen chopped garlic or 2 garlic cloves, chopped

600g/1lb 5oz mushrooms (choose a mix of chanterelle, chestnut/cremini, shiitake, porcini and brown), sliced

2 tbsp dried sliced shiitake or porcini mushrooms

2 tbsp chopped parsley leaves

350ml/12fl oz/1½ cups unsweetened almond milk

sea salt and freshly ground black pepper

MAKES 4 LUNCHES

- Heat the oil in a large saucepan over a medium heat. Add the shallots and garlic, and cook for 5 minutes until softened.

- Add the fresh and dried mushrooms, and 600ml/21fl oz/2½ cups boiling water.

- Stir well and bring to the boil, then reduce the heat and simmer for 10 minutes or until the mushrooms are cooked.

- Remove from the heat and add the parsley and almond milk. Blend the soup using a blender or food processor. Season with sea salt and plenty of black pepper.

- Divide the soup among four freezerproof containers, then cool and freeze for up to 3 months any that you don't want to eat soon. Defrost overnight in the fridge. Reheat a portion before you go to work and transfer to a vacuum food flask – or reheat it at work.

≡ TIP ≡ Dried mushrooms are a great storecupboard staple and make a rich addition to soups and stews. If you don't have any, use vegetable stock instead of the water.

★ PACKED WITH . . .

Mushrooms have been used for their immune-supportive qualities in Asian cultures for many centuries, and they are extensively researched for their cancer-preventative properties today. As a good source of energy-boosting B vitamins, iron and zinc, our fungi friends really are a wonder food.

Packed with protein from the chickpeas and lentils, this is an easy soup to make (no blending). Small, brown chickpeas are great in this soup, although any kind you have will be good. Chickpeas give a satisfying bite, so you don't need bread with this. If you have a lemon, take a wedge with you to squeeze over the hot soup; it really goes well with the spices.

SPICY CHICKPEA AND RED LENTIL SOUP

1 tbsp rapeseed/canola oil

1 red onion, chopped

1 tsp chopped frozen garlic or 1 garlic clove, chopped

½ Romano red pepper, deseeded and thinly sliced

1 tsp harissa or ½ tsp hot chilli powder, or to taste

50g/1¾oz/⅓ cup dried red lentils

200g/7oz/1 cup passata (sieved tomatoes)

100g/3½oz/heaped ¾ cup canned brown chickpeas (kala chana), rinsed and drained

sea salt and freshly ground black pepper

lemon wedges, to serve (optional)

MAKES 2 LUNCHES

• Heat the oil in a large saucepan. Add the onion, garlic and Romano pepper, and cook for 5 minutes until softened.

• Add the harissa or chilli powder and stir to coat the vegetables. Add the lentils, passata and chickpeas, and stir.

• Pour in 200ml/7fl oz/scant 1 cup water and stir well. Bring to the boil, then reduce the heat to a simmer. Cook the soup for 15 minutes or until the lentils have softened.

• Season with salt and pepper, and more harissa or chilli powder, if you like.

• Divide the soup between two freezerproof containers, then cool and freeze for up to 3 months any that you don't want to eat soon. Defrost overnight in the fridge. Reheat a portion before you go to work and transfer to a vacuum food flask – or reheat at work. Pack a lemon wedge to take with you, if using.

 TIME TO EAT   Reheat at work, if necessary, and squeeze over some lemon before eating.

★ PACKED WITH . . .

Chickpeas are a very good source of folate, a B vitamin that keeps our brain and nervous system functioning well.

MINDFUL EATING

When did we all start eating at our desks with one eye on our email? Even if we go out, it is just to queue up in a supermarket or coffee shop.

Brits are the worst in Europe at taking a proper break. It's even tougher in the USA where many people don't get paid for a lunch break, so most eat at their desks or in meetings.

Why not find somewhere you can just eat, even for just 20 minutes, and pay attention to how the food looks, how it smells and how it tastes. By noticing what you eat, you will register what you are eating, and feel more satisfied.

Take time to chew properly, and relax your body as you eat. Chewing well triggers the release of digestive enzymes in saliva that break food down and signal when you are getting full. It also means chunks of unchewed food don't enter the stomach, making you feel bloated and uncomfortable.

If you know you haven't eaten enough veggies in the last day or two, this very quick soup will fix everything. You can use frozen veg for this, but it's a great option if you have a glut in your veg box or garden. You don't need to use vegetable stock for this soup; the vegetables and lemon add plenty of flavour. The soup is best eaten on the day that it is made.

SUMMER VEGETABLE BROTH

1 tbsp rapeseed/canola oil

1 spring onion/scallion, thinly sliced

1 celery stalk, thinly sliced

50g/1¾oz/scant ½ cup frozen or fresh shelled edamame beans/green soybeans or petits pois (or use half and half)

25g/1oz/¼ cup frozen or fresh baby broad/fava beans

1 handful of fine green beans, cut in half

1 small courgette/zucchini, thinly sliced

a squeeze of lemon juice

sea salt and freshly ground black pepper

1 handful of mint leaves or rocket/arugula, stalks removed (optional), to serve

MAKES 1 LUNCH

• Heat the oil in a large saucepan and add the spring onion/scallion and celery. Cook for 5 minutes until the vegetables have softened.

• Add the edamame/green soybeans and broad/fava beans to the pan. Add 300ml/10½fl oz/1¼ cups boiling water and stir well. Bring to the boil, then reduce the heat and simmer for 5 minutes.

• Add the green beans, courgette/zucchini and lemon juice. Season with salt and plenty of black pepper.

• Transfer the soup to a vacuum food flask ready to take to work. Pack the mint leaves or rocket/arugula to take with you, if using. The beans and courgette/zucchini will cook in the hot broth.

TIME TO EAT Add the mint leaves or rocket/arugula just before eating.

★ PACKED WITH . . .

Edamame beans/green soybeans are an excellent source of plant protein as well as being rich in iron and calcium. Frozen beans are great value.

PORTABLE NOODLES

These yummy pots of goodness are simple to throw together and are the perfect way to use up veggies and other ingredients that might be lurking in your cupboards. Prepare four pots at a time, store them in the fridge and you're set up with a fresh, nutritious lunch for most of the week.

Layer flavour, protein, veggies and noodles into a sealable heatproof jar or pot and take a small tub containing your fresh toppings with you. Brown rice noodles should be eaten slightly al dente to prevent them becoming soggy – they just need boiling water to be added, so they are ideal to use for an easy lunch.

Brown rice noodles release their energy more slowly than white varieties and have a decent amount of the stress-busting mineral magnesium. Cram in plenty of fresh veggies to get at least three of your seven-a-day (see page 11).

EACH MAKES 1 LUNCH

Add all the ingredients to a 500ml/17fl oz/2 cup sealable jar or heatproof pot, apart from the optional toppings. Put in the fridge. Pack the toppings to take with you, if using. Keep the jar chilled at work, if you can, but remove it 30 minutes before you are ready to eat so that the pot comes to room temperature.

⊳TIME TO EAT⊲ Pour boiling water to just cover all the ingredients, and quickly seal. Give the jar a good shake and leave for 3–4 minutes. Stir well and add the topping, if you like.

⬅MAKE A CHANGE➡ There's no end to the different combinations of ingredients you can use in these pots. Try cooked prawns/shrimp, crab, salmon, duck or tofu as alternative proteins. What else can you find? Curry paste, fish sauce, tom yum paste, tamarind sauce and coconut cream all work well as flavourings.

TERIYAKI CHICKEN AND BROCCOLI

½ tsp frozen chopped ginger (or 5mm/¼in piece of root ginger, peeled and grated), ½ tsp chopped frozen garlic (or ½ garlic clove, chopped), ¼ deseeded and finely chopped red chilli, 1 tbsp tamari (or light soy sauce), 1 tsp honey, 50g/1¾oz dried brown rice vermicelli noodles, 1 handful of shredded cooked chicken, 1 handful of small broccoli florets, 1 small thinly sliced carrot, 2 thinly sliced mushrooms and some toasted sesame seeds (for an optional topping)

CHORIZO, COURGETTE AND RED PEPPER

½ tsp frozen chopped garlic (or ½ garlic clove, chopped), 1 tbsp tomato purée/paste, 1 tsp vegetable bouillon powder, 1 tsp smoked paprika, 50g/1¾oz dried brown rice vermicelli noodles, 50g/1¾oz sliced cooked chorizo, ¼ deseeded and sliced red pepper/bell pepper, ½ sliced courgette/zucchini, 1 tbsp frozen petits pois and some chopped basil (for an optional topping)

MUSHROOM, CASHEW AND MISO

1 tbsp brown miso paste, ½ tsp frozen chopped ginger (or 5mm/¼in piece of root ginger, peeled and grated), ½ deseeded and finely chopped red chilli, 50g/1¾oz dried brown rice vermicelli noodles, 4 sliced shiitake mushrooms (or any mushrooms that you have), 1 tbsp cashew nuts, 1 handful of shredded cavolo nero (or curly kale) and 1 chopped spring onion/scallion (for an optional topping)

★ PACKED WITH . . .

The ginger, garlic and chilli in the teriyaki noodles combine to give you a punchy anti-inflammatory boost and keep infections at bay. Paprika is rich in antioxidant carotenoids, in particular lutein and zeaxanthin, key players in eye-health, so it makes a healthy addition to the chorizo noodle pot. The brown miso paste in the mushroom noodle pot is made from fermented soybeans and brown rice and helps to populate your gut with friendly bacteria. It adds a rich, savoury taste to dishes.

This is the perfect recipe to use up your root veggies in a rejuvenating one-pot lunch for chilly days. It's packed with slow-releasing carbohydrates so you don't need any bread with this unless you have a very busy day ahead.

CHICKEN, ROOT VEGGIE AND PEARL BARLEY STEW

1 tbsp rapeseed/canola oil

400g/14oz skinless chicken breasts or skinless, boneless thighs, cut into large chunks

1 onion, chopped

1 swede/rutabaga, chopped

2 carrots, chopped

100g/3½oz/heaped ½ cup pearl barley

1 leek, sliced

1 celery stalk, chopped

4 tsp chopped frozen garlic or 4 garlic cloves, chopped

3 thyme sprigs

1 bay leaf

750ml/26fl oz/3¼ cups vegetable stock

sea salt and freshly ground black pepper

1 tsp Dijon mustard, to serve

MAKES 4 LUNCHES

• Preheat the oven to 180°C/350°F/gas 4. Heat the oil in a flameproof casserole. Add the chicken and cook for 3–4 minutes until sealed all over.

• Add all the remaining ingredients and stir well. Bring to the boil, then remove from the heat. Cover and cook in the oven for 1 hour. Check halfway through and add more water if necessary. Season with salt and pepper.

• Discard the bay leaf and thyme. Divide the stew among four freezerproof containers, then cool and freeze for up to 3 months any that you don't want to eat soon. Defrost overnight in the fridge. Reheat a portion before you go to work and transfer to a vacuum food flask – or reheat it at work. Pack the mustard in a small pot to take with you.

⏻ TIME TO EAT ⏻ Reheat at work, if necessary, and stir the mustard into the stew before eating.

★ PACKED WITH . . .

Nutty-flavoured pearl barley is rich in fibre and manganese. Manganese helps us make collagen to keep our skin and bones strong and healthy.

High in protein and low in fat, turkey is a nutritious meat and it is amazing that we don't eat it more often. Eat this chilli on its own or scoop it up with a flatbread.

TURKEY AND BLACK-EYED BEAN CHILLI

1 tbsp rapeseed/canola oil

1 red onion, chopped

1 tsp frozen chopped garlic or 1 garlic clove, chopped

1 celery stalk, chopped

450g/1lb turkey breast fillets, cut into chunks

1 tsp hot chilli powder or dried chilli/hot pepper flakes, plus extra to taste

1 tsp ground cumin

1 tsp whole cumin seeds (optional)

½ × 440g/15oz can black-eyed beans, rinsed and drained

400g/14oz can chopped tomatoes

1 green pepper/bell pepper, deseeded and cut into chunks

1 orange pepper/bell pepper, deseeded and cut into chunks

sea salt and freshly ground black pepper

lime wedges, to serve

MAKES 4 LUNCHES

- Heat the oil in a large saucepan, and add the onion, garlic and celery. Cook for 5 minutes or until softened. Add the turkey, stir, and cook for 5 minutes.

- Add the chilli, ground cumin and cumin seeds (if using). Stir well until the turkey is coated in the spices. Add 300ml/10½fl oz/ 1¼ cups water, the beans, tomatoes and peppers/bell peppers, and mix well.

- Bring the mixture to the boil, then reduce the heat to a simmer. Cook for 1½ hours or until the turkey is cooked through. Season

with salt and plenty of pepper, and add extra chilli if you like.

- Divide among four freezerproof containers, then cool and freeze for up to 3 months any that you don't want to eat soon. Defrost overnight in the fridge. Reheat a portion before you go to work and transfer to a vacuum food flask – or reheat it at work. Pack a lime wedge to take with you.

TIME TO EAT Squeeze over some lime before eating.

Black-eyed beans are full of zinc, which supports a healthy immune system, and turkey boosts mood-enhancing serotonin to help to banish the afternoon blues.

★ PACKED WITH ...

You'll get a good amount of iron from the beef and kidney beans in this chilli. Iron is crucial to help us form healthy red blood cells and keep up energy levels. Squeezing over the vitamin C-rich lemon will help absorption of this vital mineral.

This delicious chilli is perfect if you are feeling tired and need something packed with iron and vegetables, especially on a wintery day. You can eat this on its own or scoop it up with a flatbread. It's also good with cauliflower rice or rocket/arugula leaves. You'll need to make this at the weekend or when you have a few hours for it to cook slowly, but the actual work time from you is minimal.

BEEF BRISKET CHILLI

2 tbsp rapeseed/canola oil, plus extra if needed

650g/1lb 7oz beef brisket, cut into rough chunks

1 red onion, sliced

1 red pepper/bell pepper, deseeded and sliced

1 green pepper/bell pepper, deseeded and sliced

1 celery stalk, sliced

1 carrot, chopped or sliced

1 tsp frozen chopped garlic or 1 garlic clove, chopped

1 tsp ground cumin

1 tsp smoked paprika

½ tsp hot chilli powder

400g/14oz can kidney beans, rinsed and drained

1 x 400g/14oz can chopped tomatoes

sea salt and freshly ground black pepper

lime wedges, to squeeze (optional)

MAKES 4 LUNCHES

- Heat the oil in a large saucepan, then add the brisket. Cook the beef for 3–5 minutes until it starts to brown on all sides. Transfer the beef to a plate, and leave to one side.

- Add the onion, peppers, celery, carrot and garlic to the pan, with a little extra oil if needed, and cook for 5 minutes or until the vegetables start to soften and colour.

- Add the cumin and paprika, and stir well to coat the vegetables. Add the chilli powder and stir well. Add the kidney beans, tomatoes and 200ml/7fl oz/scant 1 cup water, and stir well. Bring the mixture to the boil, then reduce the heat to a simmer. Leave to cook for 3½ hours, stirring from time to time.

- Season with salt and pepper, and add more chilli, if you like. Divide the chilli among four freezerproof containers, then cool and freeze for up to 3 months any that you don't want to eat soon. Defrost overnight in the fridge. Reheat a portion before you go to work and transfer to a vacuum food flask – or reheat it at work. Pack a lime wedge to take with you, if using.

TIME TO EAT   Reheat at work, if necessary, and squeeze some lime over the chilli before eating.

This takes just a few minutes of prep and the oven does all the work. You can use frozen pre-prepped butternut squash if you like, which makes life very easy. If you want to use fresh squash, there is no need to peel the skin away before roasting it; whether you eat the skin or not is up to you. Halloumi improves upon baking, retaining its shape, absorbing surrounding flavours and adding a lovely saltiness to your lunch.

WARM ROAST VEGETABLE AND HALLOUMI SALAD

1 red pepper/bell pepper, deseeded and cut into bite-size pieces

1 green pepper/bell pepper, deseeded and cut into bite-size pieces

½ garlic bulb, broken into cloves

1 handful of cherry or baby plum tomatoes

1 red onion, cut into wedges

½ butternut squash (about 250g/9oz), unpeeled and cut into wedges

2 tbsp olive oil

1 tsp smoked paprika

250g/9oz halloumi, sliced

1 tbsp black sesame seeds

lemon wedges (optional)

freshly ground black pepper

MAKES 2–3 LUNCHES

- Preheat the oven to 200°C/400°F/gas 6. Put the red and green peppers/bell peppers, garlic, tomatoes, onion and butternut squash in a large roasting pan.

- Mix together the oil and paprika, and pour over the vegetables. Mix well to coat everything. Season with plenty of black pepper.

- Roast for 20 minutes. Remove from the oven and turn everything carefully.

- Put the halloumi on top of the vegetables and add more black pepper. Return to the oven and cook for 10 minutes or until the halloumi has softened and the edges start to brown. Remove from the oven and scatter the sesame seeds over the top.

- You can eat this cold; just remove it from the fridge about an hour before you want to eat it so that it is not ice cold. If you want to eat it warm, reheat in the morning either by putting it in a preheated oven for 5 minutes or by using a microwave on full power for 2 minutes. Transfer to a large vacuum food flask or container. Pack the lemon to take with you, if using.

TIME TO EAT Squeeze the lemon over the salad just before eating; it goes really well with the paprika. Squeeze the garlic out of its skin as you eat the salad; it is very good for you to eat it, but perhaps not if you have a big meeting.

Dhal is perfect comfort food – full of flavour, filling and great value. This lunch doesn't really need any extra carbs, but you can pack a wholemeal chapati or a couple of poppadoms to mop it up, if you like.

SWEET POTATO AND YELLOW SPLIT PEA DHAL

1 tbsp extra virgin coconut oil

1 onion, chopped

2 tsp frozen chopped garlic or 2 garlic cloves, chopped

1 tsp frozen chopped ginger

2 tsp ground turmeric

2 tsp garam masala

1 red chilli, deseeded and thinly sliced

2 sweet potatoes, scrubbed and cut into cubes

250g/9oz/scant 1¼ cups yellow split peas

400g/14oz can chopped tomatoes

sea salt

lemon wedges, for squeezing (optional)

1 handful of torn spinach leaves, to serve (optional)

MAKES 4 LUNCHES

- Heat the oil in a large saucepan over a medium heat. Add the onion and cook for 5 minutes until softened. Add the garlic, ginger, turmeric, garam masala, chilli, sweet potatoes and split peas, and stir well. Pour in the tomatoes and add 300ml/10½fl oz/ 1¼ cups water. Bring to the boil and then reduce the heat, cover and simmer for 45 minutes or until the peas are tender. Stir halfway through cooking and add more water if necessary. Season with salt.

- Divide the dhal among four freezerproof containers, then cool and freeze for up to 3 months any that you don't want to eat soon. Defrost overnight in the fridge. Reheat a portion before you go to work and transfer to a vacuum food flask – or reheat it at work. Pack the lemon and spinach to take with you, if using.

TIME TO EAT Reheat in the microwave, if necessary. Squeeze over some lemon and stir through a handful of spinach before eating.

★ PACKED WITH . . .

Split peas are a great source of slow-release energy. They also contain B vitamins that support your nervous system and help to keep you calm when stress levels are high – perfect for work.

You just need to pick up a cauliflower and an onion from the local shop on your way home for this lunch, because the rest of the ingredients can live in your freezer and cupboards for weeks on end. This curry is lovely with a flatbread or chapatti to eat alongside.

CAULIFLOWER, GREEN LENTIL AND SPINACH CURRY

2 tbsp rapeseed/canola oil

1 red onion, sliced

1 tsp frozen chopped ginger

1 tsp frozen chopped garlic, or 1 garlic clove, chopped

1 tbsp garam masala

1 tsp chilli powder

1 small cauliflower, cut into small florets

400g/14oz can chopped tomatoes

400g/14oz can green lentils, drained and rinsed

50g/1¾oz frozen whole leaf spinach

2 tbsp Greek or plain yogurt (optional)

sea salt and freshly ground black pepper

MAKES 4 LUNCHES

• Heat the oil in a large saucepan over a medium heat and add the onion, ginger, garlic, garam masala and chilli powder. Add 2 tablespoons water. Stir well. Cover and cook for 5 minutes or until the onion has softened.

• Add the cauliflower and stir well to coat in the spices. Add 150ml/5fl oz/⅔ cup boiling water and stir.

• Add the tomatoes, lentils and spinach, stir well and bring to the boil. Reduce the heat and simmer for 5 minutes. The spinach will have defrosted after this time, so give the curry a stir to mix the spinach through. Cover and cook for a further 20 minutes or until the cauliflower is just tender.

• Remove from the heat, and stir in the yogurt, if using. Season with salt and plenty of black pepper. Divide among four freezerproof containers, then cool and freeze for up to 3 months any that you don't want to eat soon. Defrost overnight in the fridge. Reheat a portion before you go to work and transfer to a vacuum food flask – or reheat it at work.

★ PACKED WITH . . .

Traditional curry ingredients such as red onion, ginger, garlic and chilli have anti-inflammatory properties which, when eaten regularly, can help reduce aches and pains, so they are great for everyone, especially if you do a lot of sport.

4. FORK-FREE MEALS

Shop-bought fish pâté often comes with added sugar and cream, and it is blended, which loses much of its texture. Making your own is far better value and so quick to make that you won't go back. This is lovely piled on hot, toasted sourdough, but if your workplace doesn't have a toaster, it goes very well with oatcakes.

TROUT, COCONUT AND LIME PÂTÉ

100g/3½oz smoked trout fillets

1 tbsp coconut yogurt

zest of 1 lime, plus a squeeze of lime juice

sea salt and freshly ground black pepper

TO SERVE
1 slice of sourdough bread, toasted, or 2–3 oatcakes

1 handful of rocket/arugula leaves

2–3 radishes, sliced

MAKES 2 LUNCHES

• Peel away any skin from the trout fillets and discard. Break the fillets into pieces using your hands. Put in a bowl.

• Add the yogurt, lime zest and juice, then use a fork to lightly mash everything together, leaving some texture. Season with a little salt and plenty of pepper. Mix well.

• Take one half to work, keeping it cool, and put the remainder in a sealed pot in the fridge – it will keep for 2 days. Pack the bread for toasting or the oatcakes to take with you.

TIME TO EAT Toast the bread and pile the pâté on top, or serve alongside oatcakes, with the rocket/arugula leaves and radishes on top.

MAKE A CHANGE Smoked mackerel is a little cheaper than trout and also works well with lime. Mash it with Greek rather than coconut yogurt, as it is a better taste combination.

★ PACKED WITH . . .

Oily fish such as trout are great sources of omega-3 fats (see page 11). We are advised to eat three servings of oily fish per week to get enough of these exceptional fats, and pâté is a no-cook way to achieve this.

This chunky, mildly sweet spread goes perfectly with bitter leaves such as chicory/
Belgian endive or with celery to scoop it up. You could also spread it on oatcakes
or a slice of pumpernickel bread, and add a few salad leaves/greens.

SWEET POTATO AND GOAT'S CHEESE DIP

**1 large sweet potato
(about 300g/10½oz)**

2 garlic cloves, chopped

**100g/3½oz soft goat's
cheese**

a squeeze of lemon juice

**1 handful of coriander/
cilantro, chopped**

1 tbsp pumpkin seeds

**salad leaves/greens,
celery or oatcakes,
to serve**

MAKES 4 LUNCHES

- Preheat the oven to 180°C/350°F/gas 4. Bake the potato
for 30 minutes or until it feels soft. Leave the potato to cool,
and then scrape out the flesh into a small bowl.

- Add the garlic, cheese, lemon juice, coriander/cilantro
and pumpkin seeds, and mash together.

- This dip will keep in the fridge for up to 3 days, or you
can freeze it for up to 3 months. Take out a portion in the
morning before work, and it will be defrosted by lunchtime.
Eat with salad leaves/greens, celery or oatcakes.

★ PACKED WITH . . .

Sweet potato is bursting with beta-carotene, which is great for
healthy skin, eyes and lungs. It also contains a good shot of
vitamin C to boost your immune system. The sweetness comes
from easily digestible sugars, which, along with the high fibre
content, will provide slow-releasing energy – perfect to see you
through the afternoon.

THINGS TO GO WITH DIPS

Packed with protein and veggies, dips can make a healthy lunch, and they are a quick option to make in the morning. Try some of the delicious recipes for dips in this chapter, then mix and match them with the suggestions below for dippers.

Crudités are an ideal way to get more veggies into your diet – plus there are lots of additional health benefits from eating them raw. If you need some carbs to go with your dip, look out for non-wheat options to vary what you eat. Make your own (see pages 153 and 171), or search out some of the great shop-bought crackers and breads now available.

BREAD

Dips also make great sandwich fillings. Spoon your dip into pitta, fill a bagel or spread on pumpernickel. Packs of flatbread and naan also freeze well and defrost in an hour or two. If you have a toaster at work, pop your bread on top to warm it through gently before eating. Other options include rye loaf, olive loaf, seeded bagel, sesame and poppy seed loaf, sourdough and spelt loaf.

BREAD CHIPS

You can use leftover tortillas, or seeded or wholemeal/whole-wheat pitta breads to make crunchy bread chips. Preheat the oven to 200°C/400°F/gas 6. If using **pitta bread**, open it out and cut it into two thin halves. Cut the **tortilla** or pitta into large triangles (scissors are great for this). Put the triangles on a baking sheet and bake for 10 minutes or until crisp. Leave to cool before putting into a container to take to work.

CRUNCHY VEGGIES

As lovely as carrot sticks are, most of us need to mix things up a bit. Here are some ideas for veggies that will still be crisp and delicious by lunchtime:

- carrots (the purple heritage variety make a good change)
- cauliflower slices or florets
- celery stalks
- cucumber wedges
- Little Gem/Bibb lettuce leaves
- radicchio leaves
- radishes
- red, orange and yellow peppers/bell peppers (deseeded and cut into thick wedges)
- sugar snap peas
- slim stalks of broccoli

GOING SHOP-BOUGHT

There are all kinds of delicious things you can buy to scoop up your dips. Choose something containing lots of seeds or made with a grain you don't usually eat, and you will add a variety of nutrients to your lunch with zero effort. Choose from:

- amaranth rice cakes
- chickpea crispbreads
- flax and pumpkin crackers
- Japanese rice crackers
- quinoa crisps
- seaweed crackers
- seeded crackers
- seeded oatcakes
- spelt and oat cakes
- spicy tortilla chips
- veggie crisps

TEAM UP . . .

Smoked trout, coconut and lime pâté + cucumber wedges

Goat's cheese and sweet potato spread + flax and pumpkin crackers

Artichoke, pine nut and olive dip + olive loaf

You can make this protein-packed dip before work in the morning – it is so quick. Mint is very easy to grow in a pot, so just grab a handful to add a fresh flavour and some vitamin C. You could pile the dip onto fresh bread with some watercress leaves on top for a summery lunch.

CANNELLINI, MINT AND LIME DIP

400g/14oz can cannellini beans, rinsed and drained

zest and juice of 1 lime

1 handful of fresh mint leaves

sea salt and freshly ground black pepper

fresh bread, crackers, breadsticks or oatcakes, to serve

1 handful of watercress leaves, to serve (optional)

MAKES 2 LUNCHES

- Tip the beans into a blender or food processor. Add the lime juice, and whizz to start blending the beans.

- Add the mint and whizz again. If the dip is too thick, add a splash of water.

- Scrape the bean dip into a bowl and stir in the lime zest. Season with salt and plenty of black pepper. Chill the dip in the fridge. It will keep for 2 days. To take to work, put a portion in a container and into a cool bag along with bread and watercress, if using, to take with you.

★ PACKED WITH . . .

In common with other white beans, cannellini beans are abundant in the essential amino acid leucine, which helps to stimulate muscle growth.

This is a chunky guacamole, packed with flavour and texture. It will be much more satisfying to eat than a tub of ready-made, which are usually too smooth. Scoop up with veggies and pitta bread chips (see page 132) or tortilla chips.

GUACAMOLE

- Scoop out the flesh of the avocado using a teaspoon into a bowl and add the tomato.

- Sprinkle over the garlic, spring onion/scallion and chilli powder, followed by the lime zest and juice. Add the coriander/cilantro and mix well, mashing the avocado a little. If using frozen garlic, it will have defrosted by lunchtime.

- Add a good pinch of salt. Transfer to a sealable container and put the avocado pit in the middle, so that it is covered by the guacamole. The pit and lime juice will stop the avocado from turning brown. Keep cold until you are ready to eat.

TIP When you buy tomatoes, leave them on a sunny windowsill to develop as much flavour as possible. There is no need to keep them in the fridge. Tomatoes should be slightly soft to the touch to use in guacamole. If you can't find a beef tomato, choose a handful of any ripe tomatoes instead.

★ PACKED WITH . . .
Feast on vitamin E-rich avocados to keep your skin smooth and blemish-free.

1 large ripe avocado, cut in half and pitted (reserve the pit)

1 ripe beef tomato, chopped

1 garlic clove, chopped

1 spring onion/scallion, sliced

½ tsp chilli powder

zest of 1 lime, plus a squeeze of lime juice

1 handful of coriander/cilantro leaves, roughly chopped

sea salt

MAKES 1 LUNCH

Bring a taste of the Mediterranean to your lunchbox with this no-fuss, tangy, green dip. There's no chopping involved so you can rustle it up in a matter of minutes. A jar of artichokes makes a really handy store cupboard ingredient to bulk up salads and sandwiches when you're running low on fresh ingredients

ARTICHOKE, SPINACH AND PINE NUT DIP

25g/1oz/2½ tbsp, plus 2 tsp, pine nuts

170g/6oz sliced artichoke hearts (from a jar), well drained

8 pitted green olives

zest and juice of 1 lemon

2 large handfuls of spinach

1 tbsp extra virgin olive oil

sea salt and freshly ground black pepper

MAKES 4 LUNCHES

• Put the 25g/1oz/2½ tbsp pine nuts in a food processor or electric chopper and add the remaining ingredients except the seasoning, then whizz until well combined but maintaining a chunky texture. Stir through the 2 teaspoons pine nuts. Season with salt and pepper.

• Divide among four separate containers and store in the fridge for up to 3 days or pour into freezerproof containers and freeze for up to 3 months any that you don't want to eat soon. Defrost overnight in the fridge.

TIP This dip is lovely rolled up inside a few slices of Parma ham/prosciutto, for some extra protein.

★ PACKED WITH . . .

The globe artichoke is a member of the thistle family and has traditionally been used to support the liver and gallbladder. It contains a natural chemical called cynarin, which helps to boost bile production and aid detoxification and digestion. This action may also help to maintain healthy cholesterol levels.

Known for their delicate, sweet flavour, tiny pine nuts are also a powerhouse of minerals, vitamins and healthy fats. They contain pinolenic acid, which may aid weight loss by triggering the release of an appetite-suppressing hormone called cholecystokinin.

Beautifully violet in colour, and sweet and earthy in taste, this dip is a delicious way to get rosy-cheeked beetroot/beets into your diet. The vacuum-packed cooked beetroot is good and it lasts for ages in the fridge, so you can whizz this up any time. Spread this dip onto oatcakes or spoon into a wholemeal/whole-wheat pitta bread with plenty of rocket/arugula and sliced spring onion/scallion.

BEETROOT AND TAHINI DIP

300g/10½oz cooked beetroot/beets, drained

4 tbsp tahini (see Tip)

2 garlic cloves, chopped

1 handful of mint leaves

4 tbsp apple cider vinegar

2 tbsp extra virgin olive oil

oatcakes, or wholemeal/ whole-wheat pitta bread, rocket/arugula and sliced spring onion/ scallion, to serve

MAKES 4 LUNCHES

- Put all the ingredients in a food processor and whizz until smooth. Put one serving in a sealed container to take to work. Chill the remainder in the fridge. It will keep for 4 days. Or divide among four freezerproof containers, and freeze for up to 3 months any that you don't want to eat soon. Defrost overnight in the fridge. Pack the oatcakes, rocket/arugula and spring onion/scallion to take with you.

TIP Tahini is a sesame seed paste used in Middle Eastern dishes. It's great in dips, but you can also add it to salad dressings, pasta sauces, flapjacks and granola.

★ PACKED WITH . . .

As well as iron and folic acid, beetroot/beet is also high in fibre.

Athletes should include plenty of beetroot/beet in their diet, as its nitrate content can boost endurance and stamina. Beetroot juice is another way to up your nitrate intake.

Yes, hummus can be bought everywhere, but making your own means you know exactly what is in it. It is so quick that you can make it in the morning before work (leave the washing-up until later). The texture of homemade hummus is far more interesting than shop-bought, especially if you leave a few chickpeas whole. Tahini adds depth of flavour, but this recipe tastes great without it, so don't feel you need to buy a jar just for this; you can also add different ingredients to mix things up a bit (see Make a Change, below).

ROASTED RED PEPPER HUMMUS

400g/14oz can chickpeas, rinsed and drained

1 tbsp olive oil

1 roasted pepper from a jar, cut into rough chunks

1 garlic clove, chopped

1 tsp tahini (optional)

zest of 1 lemon, plus a squeeze of juice

sea salt and freshly ground black pepper

wholemeal/whole-wheat pitta bread and rocket/arugula, to serve

MAKES 4 LUNCHES

• Tip the chickpeas into a blender or food processor, and add the oil, pepper, garlic, tahini, if using, and lemon zest and juice.

• Whizz everything together until well combined, but with some texture remaining. If you need to, add 1–2 tablespoons water to help it whizz around.

• Scrape out the hummus into a bowl. Add salt and plenty of black pepper, and check the taste. Add a little more lemon juice, if you like.

• Serve this spooned inside pitta breads (warmed in a toaster if you can), and stuffed with plenty of rocket/arugula leaves. Warming the pitta breads makes them easier to open; let them cool before you fill them. The hummus will keep for 3 days in the fridge.

← MAKE A CHANGE → Instead of roasted pepper, try these variations. You will need to add a little more olive oil to blend the mixture (use the oil from the jar):

• 4 large sun-dried tomatoes in oil

• 2 preserved artichokes, in oil. Chop them roughly before adding to the blender or food processor

• 25g/1oz/¼ cup pitted Kalamata (purple) olives, in oil

★ PACKED WITH ...

Tahini is an excellent vegan source of bone-strengthening calcium and fertility-boosting zinc.

You can eat this on its own, or piled into a wholemeal/whole-wheat wrap or pitta bread, or add some shredded chicken or tuna. Many shop-bought salsas have added sugar, which diminishes the nutrient content and overwhelms the delicious fresh flavour of the ingredients. Avocado can go brown if you prepare it hours in advance, so pack it alongside the rest of the salad and add it at lunchtime.

AVOCADO, CUCUMBER AND MANGO SALSA

½ **red pepper/bell pepper, deseeded and diced**

5cm/2in piece of **cucumber, diced**

4 **cherry tomatoes, cut into quarters**

½ **mango, diced**

1 **spring onion/scallion, sliced**

¼ **red chilli, deseeded and finely chopped**

squeeze of **lime juice**

1 small **avocado**

wholemeal/whole-wheat wrap or pitta bread, to serve (optional)

MAKES 1 LUNCH

• Gently mix together all the ingredients, apart from the avocado, in a bowl. Transfer to a sealed container to take to work.

▰ TIME TO EAT ▰ When you are ready to eat the salsa, cut open the avocado, discard the pit, and, using a teaspoon, scoop out chunks on to your salsa. Mix in gently. Spoon into a wrap to eat, if you like.

★ PACKED WITH . . .

Red peppers/bell peppers are bursting with immune-boosting beta-carotene and vitamin C, to help you to fight off infections. By eating them raw you'll get a really good dose of these vital nutrients.

This delicious open sandwich is just the thing when you feel like something special at lunchtime. Toasting the bread before you make the sandwich improves the flavour and prevents it getting a soggy bottom. Pumpernickel bread is very filling, so you'll need only one slice for this lunch.

CRAYFISH AND AVO OPEN SANDWICH

1 thick slice of pumpernickel bread

75g/2½oz cooked crayfish tails

zest of ½ lemon

a squeeze of lemon juice

1 tsp plain yogurt

1 handful of watercress

1 small ripe avocado

freshly ground black pepper

MAKES 1 SANDWICH

• Toast the bread and leave to cool. Meanwhile, put the crayfish in a small bowl and add the lemon zest and juice and yogurt. Season with plenty of black pepper and mix well.

• Put the pumpernickel bread onto a large square of baking parchment. Spoon over the crayfish mix and top with the watercress. Wrap this up in the parchment and secure with an elastic band. Put into a sealable container with the avocado.

TIME TO EAT   Cut the avocado in half, remove the pit and scoop the flesh onto the sandwich using a teaspoon.

TIP   Treat yourself to seafood such as prawns/shrimp, crayfish or fresh crab occasionally. Not only do they taste great but they're also packed with nutrients. Even buying a fresh prepared crab is cheaper than many pre-packed salads from the high-street chains.

★ PACKED WITH . . .

In this sandwich you'll get a perfect mix of protein, heart-healthy fats, vitamin C and slow-releasing carbohydrates. As well as containing protein, crayfish is rich in selenium, a powerful antioxidant that supports immune function and helps to power your thyroid.

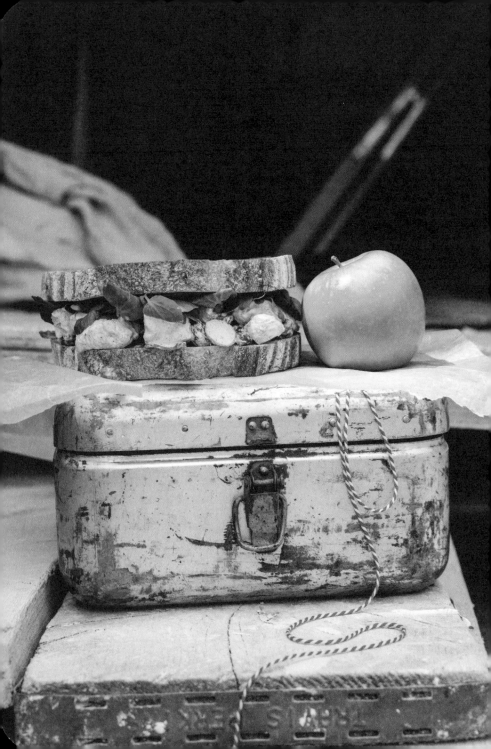

This is such an easy way to cook juicy chicken that you will never buy those packs of cooked chicken again. You can buy organic, free-range chicken for the price of the ready cooked, and there are no additives. Double up the quantity of chicken if you like, to use in a salad another day. Greek yogurt is a lighter alternative to shop-bought mayonnaise.

CORONATION-ISH CHICKEN SANDWICH

100g/3½oz chicken breast fillet, cut into chunks

1 tsp frozen chopped ginger or 1cm/½in piece of root ginger, peeled and grated

1 tsp sultanas/golden raisins

2 slices of rye or sourdough bread

1 tsp Greek yogurt

½ tsp medium curry powder or garam masala

3 radishes, sliced

1 handful of watercress, stalks removed

sea salt and freshly ground black pepper

MAKES 1 SANDWICH

- Put the chicken, ginger, sultanas/golden raisins and plenty of black pepper in a saucepan and cover with boiling water. Bring to the boil, then remove from the heat, cover and leave for 5 minutes.

- Test the chicken is cooked through by pulling apart the largest piece. Drain the chicken and sultanas/golden raisins, then leave to cool.

- Toast the bread, and leave to one side. Mix together the yogurt and curry powder, then add the radishes and the cooled chicken and sultanas/golden raisins. Stir well, and season with salt and more black pepper, if needed.

- Spoon the chicken mixture onto a slice of bread, top with watercress, then add the other slice of bread. Wrap up in baking parchment and secure with an elastic band or string. Put into a sealable container ready to take to work.

★ PACKED WITH . . .

Curry powder and garam masala provide an anti-inflammatory mix of turmeric, chilli powder, ground coriander, ground cumin, ground ginger and pepper.

Most take-out beef sandwiches are piled high with meat and lack vegetables; this is a more balanced suggestion for you. Sauerkraut is super-cheap to buy, healthy and it also goes really well with beef. Salt beef is also delicious with the Celeriac Slaw on page 86.

SALT BEEF AND SAUERKRAUT SANDWICH

2 thick slices of rye bread

2 tsp American or Dijon mustard

1 handful of rocket/ arugula leaves

2 slices of salt beef (about 75g/2½oz)

1 tbsp sauerkraut

MAKES 1 SANDWICH

- Toast the rye bread lightly on both sides. Leave to cool while you get the other ingredients ready.

- Spread the mustard thinly on each slice of toast. Put the rocket/arugula leaves on one slice, followed by the beef and sauerkraut.

- Top with the second piece of toast. Wrap this up in baking parchment and secure with an elastic band. Put into a sealable container. Keep cold until you are ready to eat.

TIP Sauerkraut is made with just cabbage and salt. It is pretty easy to make yourself, but as jars are so cheap, it's worth buying a couple to keep in the cupboard. Look for jars with as few ingredients as possible: cabbage, salt and possibly juniper berries, which are a traditional flavouring. Most supermarkets and Polish delis sell a good range. Once your jar is open, keep it in the fridge.

★ PACKED WITH . . .

Sauerkraut is rich in healthy bacteria, which help to keep your gut happy.

Inspired by the bright colours of summer veggies, this super-fresh sandwich will help you get your seven-a-day. If you can't find millet or buckwheat bread, feel free to pack all the ingredients into a toasted wholemeal pitta bread or pile on to grainy bread.

SUMMER GARDEN SANDWICH

2 slices of millet or buckwheat bread

1 small raw beetroot/beet

1 radish

1 small carrot

½ small courgette/zucchini

1 spring onion/scallion, finely sliced

FOR THE PESTO
1 handful of rocket/arugula

4 almonds

a squeeze of lemon juice

1 tbsp extra virgin olive oil

2 sun-dried tomatoes

1 garlic clove, chopped (optional)

a pinch each of sea salt and freshly ground black pepper

MAKES 1 SANDWICH

- Toast the bread, if wished, and leave it to cool. To make the pesto, put all the ingredients into a food processor and whizz until well combined but still a little chunky.

- Spread one side of each slice of bread with pesto. Put one slice, pesto-side up, onto a large sheet of baking parchment.

- Use a vegetable peeler to cut ribbons of beetroot/beets, radish, carrot and courgette/zucchini directly onto the bread. Scatter over the spring onion/scallion.

- Top with the other slice of bread, pesto-side down. Wrap the sandwich in the baking parchment and secure with an elastic band. Put in a sealable container.

TIP Rocket/arugula pesto is very good in this sandwich but do experiment with other greens such as spinach, watercress, kale, basil, mint or coriander/cilantro. You could also buy ready-made pesto, but aim for a fresh tub rather than a jar, if you can. You can easily increase the quantities used here and store the pesto in the fridge for up to 1 week or freeze what you don't use for up to 3 months.

★ PACKED WITH . . .

Highly nutritious, rocket/arugula is particularly rich in vitamins A and C, and folic acid. It is very easy to grow in the garden or in a pot on the windowsill during the summer months. Cut it regularly and watch it keep growing back for a month or so.

Millions of sandwiches are sold every day, with research showing that some people eat a sandwich (sometimes exactly the same type) each day! We get it: they are easy to find and easy to eat. The bread that gets used in mass-made sandwiches is not doing you any favours, though; it is over-processed, sweetened and pretty devoid of nutrients.

BETTER BREAD

There are plenty of alternatives to the standard sandwich lunch in this book, but sometimes only bread will do. Why not try just one or two bread-based lunches per week? If you like to eat toast for breakfast, aim to eat something other than bread at lunch, for variety if nothing else.

BREAD TIPS

• White bread has little to recommend it, as all the fibre and nutrients have been processed out, so try to avoid it. A chunk of crusty white baguette will have the same impact on your blood sugar as a can of cola, and you'll soon feel hungry again. Step away from the mass-produced white sliced.

• If you can, buy fresh bread from an indie bakery, which should be much lower in sugar, salt and additives than the mass-produced varieties. The supermarket instore bakeries use mixes that have nothing in common with homemade bread.

• Spend more and eat less. Treat yourself and buy a loaf of seed-packed bread. Cut it into wedges, and freeze. Just take out one piece when you need it to take to work. There is an argument that your body gets bored if you eat the same things regularly and you hardly notice eating them; trying some new breads should mean

you 'register' them more, and feel more satisfied. The wedges of bread sold to go with soup in takeouts are pretty expensive. You can save money by taking your own.

• German-style breads such as sonnenbrot, pumpernickel or volkenbrot are jam-packed with whole grains and are really satisfying. They taste better lightly toasted before you use them in a sandwich (toasting also stops them from falling apart).

• Sourdough rye breads are often easier to digest than wheat-based breads, and are substantial, fibre-rich and delicious. Rye releases its energy slowly and is higher in zinc than wheat.

• Look out for bread with added oats and barley, as they are slow-releasing grains.

• Why not make open sandwiches where you use only one slice of bread? Pile it high with toppings! (See page 145 for Crayfish and Avo Open Sandwich.)

This quick-to-make, protein-rich flatbread is super-filling. You can make a batch at the weekend to last you a few days. You can also vary your flatbreads by adding chilli/hot pepper flakes, garlic, sun-dried tomatoes or herbs.

CHICKPEA AND TURMERIC FLATBREADS

150g/5½oz/scant 1¼ cups chickpea (gram) flour

½ tsp ground turmeric

1 tsp extra virgin coconut oil

sea salt and freshly ground black pepper

MAKES 4 FLATBREADS

- Put the flour into a bowl. Gradually add 300ml/10½fl oz/1¼ cups water, beating with a fork as you go. Cover with cling film/plastic wrap and leave for 1 hour or overnight.

- Add the turmeric, salt and plenty of black pepper and stir well.

- Melt the coconut oil in a small frying pan over a medium heat. Pour in a quarter of the batter. Cook for 2–3 minutes until the base is well browned, then flip it over. Cook for another 2–3 minutes until the base is slightly charred. Remove from the pan to cool. Repeat with the remaining mixture. Store the flatbreads in an airtight container in a cool place for up to 2 days. Freeze, separated with parchment, for up to 3 months.

GLUTEN FREE? Not all gluten-free breads are that great for you. Look for millet or buckwheat loaves and avoid processed gluten-free breads packed with additives. Or make your own using nut and seed flours.

★ PACKED WITH . . .

Chickpea (gram) flour makes this a gluten-free flatbread that is rich in protein.

DELI PLATES

This page is all about good shopping so you have a shelf full of ingredients that you can pick from to make a nutritious lunch. Juicy olives, roasted artichokes and peppers – a few of these packed in a container with a chunk of bread and a slice of ham is going to be far more delicious than a mass-produced sandwich from the canteen or petrol station. Add whatever salad veggies you have in the fridge, and this becomes an easy, no-cook lunch. Use a bento or tiffin box, or something with dividers to keep things separate.

PRESERVED FISH

Look further than basic cans of tuna and seek out smoked, pickled and marinated fish, such as roll-mop herrings or pickled anchovies. Packs of smoked fish last well over a week, and jars and cans will last for months. Choose fish in olive oil where possible; the fish will be much juicier, and the oil helps you absorb the nutrients. Choose from anchovies, crayfish, herrings, kippers, mackerel,

CHARCUTERIE

You only need a few slices of smoked or cured meat to get a hit of flavour. Why not aim to eat meat at lunch only once a week and make it something really delicious, rather than, say, mass-produced ham. Check the packaging before buying to avoid too many preservatives – some have a very long list. Choose from cured chorizo, Parma ham/prosciutto, roast ham, salami, smoked duck or speck.

LOVE YOUR LEFTOVERS

There are plenty of recipes in the book that will make a good addition to your deli plate, such as Lemony Lamb Koftas (page 158), Paleo Frittata (page 43), Roasted Red Pepper Hummus (page 142), Warm Roast Vegetable and Halloumi Salad (page 122) and Slaws (pages 86–7).

PICKLES

Pickled vegetables are delicious and fine in moderation, especially if you avoid any made with loads of sugar. Rinse them first to remove the excess sugar and sharpness, if you like. Choose from beetroot/beets, cornichons, cucumbers, onions, shallots and red cabbage.

DRIED FRUIT

Lovely with cheese, and less sugary than chutney, dried fruit adds contrast to your lunch. Include a small handful and choose from apricots, apples, dates, sultanas/golden raisins and figs.

PRESERVED VEGETABLES AND PULSES

Mediterranean veggies are full of flavour and vitamins, so it's lovely to eat them all year round. Buy them in olive oil, drain off the excess and enjoy them squished onto crusty bread. Choose from butter beans, olive tapenade, olives, roasted artichokes, roasted aubergines/eggplant, roasted peppers/bell peppers, sauerkraut and sun-dried tomatoes.

CHEESES

There is absolutely nothing wrong with bread and cheese for lunch, but make it delicious and interesting. Don't buy a big pack of Cheddar or Monterey Jack every week; instead, swap it for juicy feta, a tangy blue cheese or something new from your local deli. If you choose something new, interesting and strong in flavour, you won't feel the need to eat as much. Delicate cheeses such as mozzarella are delicious with fresh tomatoes and are far nicer than buying the basic cheese sarnie from the supermarket. Choose from blue cheeses, feta, goat's cheese, Gouda, Manchego, mozzarella, burrata, Stilton or Wensleydale.

NUTS

Add a small handful of whole almonds, pistachio nuts, walnuts or anything you choose, for some protein-packed crunch. Nuts go so well with cheese and preserved vegetables, and you will often find them in tapas bars alongside chorizo and frittata, so why not add a few to your lunch?

If your stamina is flagging at the end of a busy week, you might need to up the protein and iron in your diet, and these koftas are the perfect way to do so. The koftas can be eaten hot or cold and are delicious with the mint and yogurt dip, a wholemeal/whole-wheat pitta bread and plenty of green salad. Toast your pitta at work, if you can, as it is lovely warm and with a little crunch.

LEMONY LAMB KOFTAS WITH MINT AND YOGURT DIP

250g/9oz/heaped 1 cup minced/ground lamb

½ red onion, thinly sliced

2 tsp frozen chopped garlic or 2 garlic cloves, chopped

1 tsp ground cinnamon

a pinch of freshly grated nutmeg

zest of 1 lemon

1 tsp sea salt

freshly ground black pepper

wholemeal/whole-wheat pitta bread and green salad, to serve

FOR THE MINT AND YOGURT DIP
150g/5½oz/heaped ⅔ cup Greek yogurt

juice and zest of ½ lemon

1 tbsp mint leaves, finely chopped

a pinch of salt

MAKES 2 LUNCHES

• Preheat the grill/broiler. Put the lamb and the remaining ingredients in a bowl and mix well using your hands. Roll the mixture into 12 walnut-size balls.

• Put the koftas in a baking pan and put under the grill/broiler for 5 minutes. Turn the koftas and cook for a further 5 minutes until they are browned. Check the meat is cooked through by breaking one open.

• Meanwhile, stir all the ingredients for the mint and yogurt dip together in a bowl. Transfer to two sealed containers and keep cool until needed.

• Leave the koftas to cool before storing them in a sealed container in the fridge for up to 3 days. The koftas also freeze well for up to 3 months. Defrost overnight in the fridge. Pack the dip, bread and salad to take with you.

▰ TIME TO EAT ▰ If you'd prefer to eat the koftas warm, put them in the microwave at work at full power for 1–2 minutes.

★ PACKED WITH . . .

Grass-fed lamb has notable amounts of heart-friendly omega-3 fats compared to other red meats. It is iron rich and a good source of B vitamins, particularly mood-enhancing and energy-boosting B_{12}.

SATISFYING SUSHI ROLLS

These nutritious brown rice sushi rolls are simple to make once you've got the knack. You will need a bamboo rolling mat, but they aren't expensive, and you can buy them online. It's also worth investing in a bento-style box with compartments to transport your sushi and accompaniments neatly. It's lovely to open the box at lunchtime to find these colourful rolls and dive in with your chopsticks. For a truly authentic experience, make yourself a cup of instant miso soup or green tea to enjoy with the sushi.

SUSHI ROLL BASE

Put **50g/1¾oz/heaped ¼ cup brown basmati rice** in a saucepan and add **500ml/17fl oz/2 cups water** and a **pinch of sea salt**. Bring to the boil, reduce the heat and simmer for 25–30 minutes until the rice is tender and all the water is absorbed (check from time to time and add more water if necessary). Once cooked, stir through **2 tsp brown rice vinegar**. Taste, and add more salt or vinegar if needed.

MAKES 1 LUNCH

TIP Nori is dried and roasted seaweed and is a daily staple of the Japanese diet. Seaweed is an excellent source of iodine, which plays a vital role in your body's hormonal system. It is essential to make the thyroid hormone that is responsible for powering metabolism. An underactive thyroid is linked with weight gain, fatigue and a low sex drive. Seaweed also provides a whole raft of essential and easily absorbable minerals and vitamins, and we could all benefit from including it in our diet every now and again.

CHOOSE YOUR FILLING

PRAWN AND CUCUMBER FILLING

2 tbsp cooked, peeled prawns/shrimp, **6 strips of cucumber 1cm/½in thick**, and **1 tsp sesame seeds**.

TUNA AND MANGO FILLING

2 tbsp drained canned tuna in spring water, **¼ mango**, cut into strips, and **¼ deseeded and finely chopped red chilli**.

SHIITAKE MUSHROOM AND CREAM CHEESE FILLING

4 chopped shiitake mushrooms, **1 handful of watercress**, roughly chopped, and **1 tbsp cream cheese**

CRAB AND AVOCADO FILLING

2 tbsp white crab meat, **¼ avocado**, cut into strips, **½ deseeded and finely chopped red chilli**, and a **squeeze of lime juice**.

🥢 TIP 🥢 If you're cooking rice for dinner, throw a little extra into the pan to use to make sushi rolls for the next day. Just be sure to cool it properly: spread it out on a plate so that it cools quickly, and, once cool, put it in the fridge.

ADD THE FILLING

Put a bamboo rolling mat on a work surface with the slats running horizontally to you. Put 1 sheet of nori, shiny-side down, on the mat. Spread the rice evenly over the nori, leaving 2cm/¾in clear at the top.

Arrange your filling choice in even strips across the rice, starting 1cm/½in from the edge nearest to you.

Begin rolling the mat from the edge closest to you, holding the filling in place with your fingers. Roll firmly but not so hard that the filling starts to escape. When you reach the end, squeeze the roll gently to secure the ingredients.

Put the roll on a chopping board. Cut into six slices, each about 3cm/1¼in wide, using a sharp, wet knife.

Put the sushi into a bento box or sealed container. If you like, pack soy sauce or tamari (gluten-free soy sauce), pickled ginger and wasabi paste, to accompany the sushi.

The sushi will keep overnight in the fridge and should be kept chilled until lunchtime.

5. SNACKS AND BITES

Can't resist a crunchy, salty snack? Keep a tub of these in your bag for a nutrition boost. Kale isn't to everyone's taste, but prepared this way it's irresistible. The recipe uses cavolo nero (black kale). It's more robust than curly kale and won't burn as easily. The secret is to dry out the kale rather than cooking it so that it retains its goodness and doesn't burn (so don't be tempted to turn up the heat).

TAMARI AND LIME KALE CRISPS

150g/5½oz cavolo nero, stalks removed

2 tsp extra virgin olive oil

a good squeeze of lime juice

2 tsp tamari or light soy sauce

a pinch of sea salt

MAKES 5 SNACKS

- Preheat the oven to 80°C/176°F/gas ¼. Dry the washed cavolo nero well using a clean cloth or paper towels, then cut it into crisp-size pieces. Put in a large bowl.

- Massage the oil into the cavolo nero using your hands so that it is well coated. Add the lime juice and tamari, and mix again with your hands to distribute the flavourings evenly.

- Layer thinly over 2 large baking sheets and put in the oven for 45 minutes until nicely crisp. Check regularly to ensure that it doesn't burn.

- Turn off the oven and leave the crisps inside to cool. Once cool, sprinkle with salt and transfer to an airtight container. Store for up to 1 week in a cool, dark place. To take to work, put a couple of handfuls in a small container – avoid bags, as the crisps might crumble.

← MAKE A CHANGE → Experiment with your own flavours – apple cider vinegar, celery salt, chilli/hot pepper flakes and paprika work well.

★ PACKED WITH . . .

Kale truly deserves its time in the spotlight. Packed with a host of nutrients including vitamin C, beta-carotene, iron, calcium and vitamin K, it helps to boost energy and the immune system and keep bones strong and healthy.

Simple to make, these delicious bites are the perfect snack to see you through a busy afternoon. You can also add them to salads and soup for some added crunch.

SPICY POPPED CHICKPEAS

400g/14oz can chickpeas, rinsed and drained

1 tbsp olive oil

2 tsp ras-el-hanout

sea salt

MAKES 4 SNACKS

- Preheat the oven to 200°C/400°F/gas 6. Dry the chickpeas thoroughly using paper towels.

- Put the chickpeas, olive oil and ras-el-hanout in a bowl, and mix well using your hands.

- Spread the chickpeas over a large baking pan and put in the middle of the oven for 25–30 minutes until crispy. Check regularly to make sure they don't burn.

- Remove from the oven and season with salt to taste. Allow to cool, then store in an airtight container in a cool dark place for up to 5 days. To take to work, tip a portion into a sealable container.

★ PACKED WITH . . .

The humble chickpea is a great veggie source of iron, protein and fibre.

≡ TIP ≡

Ras-el-hanout is a North African blend of spices. If you don't have any in the cupboard try ground cumin, cinnamon, coriander or chilli.

SHOPPING LIST SUPERSTARS

If you have a supply of these in your kitchen, you will always be able to make something for lunch. Everything here lasts for at least a week, so just do an online shop at the weekend and you will be ready to make your own nutrition-packed lunch.

CUPBOARD
Almonds • borlotti/cranberry beans • cashews • chickpeas • cooked lentils • eggs • extra virgin olive oil • kidney beans • olives • roasted artichokes • roasted peppers • sardines in tomato sauce • tuna in olive oil

FRIDGE
Chorizo • courgettes/zucchini • feta cheese • halloumi cheese • Parma ham/prosciutto • rocket/arugula • romano peppers

FREEZER
Edamame beans/green soybeans • peas • sweetcorn

WINDOWSILL
Cress • mint • lemons • limes

Potato crisps might be tempting, but they'll rarely leave you feeling satisfied for long. These delicious quinoa crisps are packed full of fibre, protein and healthy fats, so you won't be reaching for another snack later. Eat these crisps on their own, or with hummus, salsa or guacamole (see chapter 4). Experiment with your own choice of herbs and spices to vary the flavour: celery salt or fennel seeds work well.

QUINOA AND CHILLI CRISPS

100g/3½oz/heaped ½ cup quinoa

50g/1¾oz/⅓ cup chia seeds

1 tsp sea salt

3 tbsp pumpkin seeds

50g/1¾oz/5⅔ tbsp sesame seeds

1 tsp nigella seeds

2 tsp dried chilli/hot pepper flakes

freshly ground black pepper

MAKES 5 SNACKS

• Preheat the oven to 160°C/315°F/gas 2½. Line a large baking sheet with baking parchment. Put the quinoa in a saucepan with 200ml/7fl oz/¾ cup water, bring to the boil, then reduce the heat, cover and simmer until all the water is absorbed and the quinoa is soft and fluffy. Leave to cool.

• Meanwhile, mix the chia seeds and 150ml/5fl oz/scant ⅔ cup water together in a bowl, using a fork, then leave to stand for 5 minutes or until it forms a thick porridge-/oatmeal-like consistency.

• Stir the quinoa into the chia mixture followed by the salt, seeds, chilli/hot pepper flakes and plenty of black pepper.

• Spread the mixture over the prepared baking sheet as thinly as you can. Bake for 30 minutes. Cut into 5cm/2in squares and carefully turn each crisp over.

• Return to the oven for another 20–30 minutes until golden and set; check them regularly to make sure that they don't burn.

• Remove from the oven and leave to cool completely on the sheet. Store in a sealed container. The crisps will keep for up to 1 week. To take to work, transfer a portion to a sealable container.

★ PACKED WITH . . .

Quinoa provides the full spectrum of stress-busting B vitamins to help you stay on top form throughout the day.

NOURISHING NIBBLES

As a rule, we don't recommend too much snacking. If you find that you need lots of snacks, you might need to think whether your breakfast and lunch are substantial enough.

Constant grazing, even on healthy foods such as fruit, nuts and seeds, elevates insulin levels throughout the day, which encourages abdominal fat and increases the risk of heart disease. That said, if you have a long, hectic day ahead, packing one or two nutritious snacks will keep you away from the vending machine.

An ideal snack combines complex carbohydrate with a little protein to provide you with a gentle and long-lasting supply of energy.

SIMPLE CHIA SNACK POT

You can make this the night before, or in the morning – just keep it in the fridge for about 2 hours until ready to eat and it will set.

MAKES 1 SNACK

Put **2 tbsp chia seeds** into a small sealable pot and add **125ml/4fl oz/½ cup unsweetened almond milk**, **½ tsp xylitol** and **¼ tsp vanilla extract**. Put the lid on firmly. Shake very well for 30 seconds. Chill overnight in the fridge or take to work and put in the fridge – it will be set in a few hours.

TIME TO EAT Cut open **1 passion fruit** and scoop out the seedy pulp on top of the chia mixture.

★ PACKED WITH . . . Small but mighty chia seeds are loaded with fibre, protein, omega-3 fats and certain B vitamins to help you power through your day.

⚑ SNACK POTS ⚑

- Hard-boiled egg and a handful of cherry tomatoes
- A few squares of dark chocolate, dried cherries and a small handful of almonds
- Cubed watermelon and feta cheese
- Olives and sun-dried tomatoes
- A small can of tuna, drained, mixed with chopped celery, cucumber and spring onion/scallion
- 1 handful of Good-For-You Granola (see page 34)
- 3 chopped dates with 3 Brazil nuts
- 3 chopped dried figs and a small handful of walnuts
- 3 chopped dried apricots and a small handful of macadamia nuts
- 1 celery stalk, cut into short lengths, spread with unsweetened nut butter
- 1 handful of leftover roast chicken and 1 celery stalk, chopped

- 1 handful of Spicy Roasted Seed Mix (see page 96)
- Chopped veggies or oatcakes with any of the dips on pages 131–144
- Oatcakes sandwiched with nut butter and sugar-free jam
- A small tub of plain yogurt with 1 small banana, sliced
- Ham and cucumber slices on a rye crispbread
- A small avocado, cut in half, pitted and sprinkled with 1 tsp mixed seeds and a squeeze of lime
- A small can of sardines with cucumber slices
- A sachet of miso soup – just put it in a mug and pour over some boiling water
- Chicory/Belgian endive leaves with a small pot of cottage cheese

THINK AHEAD: If you like to snack on nuts or seeds, it's sensible to pack a small portion each day so that you will avoid mindlessly munching through a bagful.

⚑ MINDFUL SNACKING ⚑

Take 5 minutes to focus on chewing and enjoying your snack so that you can really feel the benefits. Leave your desk if you can.

When popcorn is home prepared without loads of oil, sugar and salt, it's a good high-fibre snack. It's pretty low in calories and carbs too, so you can munch this in the afternoon without feeling sluggish afterwards.

PAPRIKA POPCORN

1 tsp extra virgin coconut oil

50g/1¾oz/¼ cup popping corn kernels

1 tbsp butter

1 tsp smoked paprika

MAKES 2 BAGFULS

- Use a large saucepan with a see-through lid. Heat the oil in the pan over a medium heat until it melts and covers the base of the pan. Tip in the corn and toss to coat in the oil. Put the lid on.

- It can take up to 5 minutes for the corn to start popping, so shake the pan every minute or so to prevent the corn burning. When the corn starts to pop, it then takes only a minute or two to fill the pan with popcorn. When you can't hear any more popping, tip the popcorn into a bowl.

- Put the butter and smoked paprika in the pan, and stir well until the butter melts. Turn off the heat. Tip the popcorn back into the pan, and stir well to coat in the butter sauce.

- Leave to cool before tipping the corn into a bag or container to take to work. The popcorn will last for up to 3 days in an airtight container.

← MAKE A CHANGE → For Salted Honey Popcorn, omit the paprika and replace with 1 tbsp honey and 1 tsp sea salt.

★ PACKED WITH . . .

Corn contains a good amount of B vitamins as well as protein and fibre, so it helps to keep blood sugar levels stable.

A slice of this cake, packed with seeds and fruit, is an option for breakfast and is a good choice if it is your turn to make a cake for the office. The seed and grain flour in this recipe contains millet grains and flaxseeds, but using all self-raising flour will work too.

BANANA, APRICOT AND PUMPKIN SEED LOAF

100g/3½oz/7 tbsp butter, softened

75g/2½oz/heaped ⅓ cup golden caster/superfine sugar

2 eggs

100g/3½oz/⅔ cup dried apricots, chopped

3 tbsp pumpkin seeds

100g/3½oz/¾ cup seed and grain flour

100g/3½oz/¾ cup self-raising/self-rising flour

1 tsp baking powder

2 large or 3 small bananas (about 400g/14oz unpeeled)

60ml/2fl oz/¼ cup milk of your choice

MAKES 1 LOAF, 10 SLICES

- Preheat the oven to 170°C/325°F/gas 3. Put a paper loaf case inside a 900g/2lb loaf pan, or butter and flour the pan.

- In a large mixing bowl, cream together the butter and sugar until soft and fluffy.

- Break in the eggs and mix them gently into the butter mixture. Tip in the apricots and pumpkin seeds, and stir.

- Sift the flours and baking powder into the mixture; the seeds and grains will collect in the sieve/sifter, so just tip them in when you finish sieving.

- In a separate bowl, mash together the bananas, then add them to the mixture. Stir well to combine. Add the milk, and stir well. Spoon the mixture into the prepared loaf pan.

- Bake the loaf for 45 minutes or until golden. Check that the loaf is cooked by inserting a skewer into the centre; if it comes out clean, the loaf is done. If not, cook for another 5 minutes, and test again.

- Remove the loaf from the pan still in the paper case, and leave to cool. When the loaf is totally cold, wrap it in foil or put it in a cake tin. You can cut it into thick slices and freeze it for up to 2 months, if you like.

★ PACKED WITH . . .

Apricots contain beta-carotene and vitamin E, which can protect skin from sun damage. Most dried apricots are preserved with sulfur dioxide, a preservative that can cause health problems, so choose the unsulfured ones that are usually not bright orange.

This recipe was originally designed for clients who wanted something healthy and satisfying to munch with their mid-morning or afternoon cup of tea. It's full of healthy ingredients with a base of mood-boosting rolled oats and just a touch of sugar to keep the glycaemic load down (see page 10). Feel free to try your own combination of nuts, seeds and dried fruit.

GOOD MOOD COOKIES

- Preheat the oven to 180°C/350°F/gas 4. Line a large baking sheet with baking parchment. Put the rolled oats in a saucepan and add the coconut oil and sugar. Heat over a medium heat until the oil has melted and everything is well combined. Leave to cool slightly, and then stir in the remaining ingredients.

- Use your hands to form and squeeze the mixture into walnut-size balls and put on the baking sheet. Squash them down gently using a fork. The mixture can be quite crumbly, so use your fingers to press it back together.

- Bake for 12–15 minutes until golden. Leave to cool on the baking sheet for 5 minutes, then lift off the cookies using a palette knife on to a wire/cooling rack, and leave to cool completely.

- The cookies will keep for up to 1 week in an airtight container. To take just one or two to work, wrap in foil or baking parchment.

150g/5½oz/1½ cups jumbo/ rolled oats

50g/1¾oz/¼ cup extra virgin coconut oil

50g/1¾oz/¼ cup light muscovado sugar

1 large egg, beaten

3 tbsp pumpkin seeds

25g/1oz/scant ¼ cup Brazil nuts, roughly chopped

3 tbsp sunflower seeds

50g/1¾oz/⅓ cup dried apricots, roughly chopped

MAKES 12 COOKIES

★ PACKED WITH . . .

Rolled oats release their energy slowly and are rich in vitamin B$_6$, which helps raise your serotonin levels and boost your mood. Pumpkin seeds contain zinc, which boosts immunity and gives a healthy glow to your skin. Brazil nuts and dried apricots are rich in calcium for strong bones and teeth.

Antioxidant-rich dried cherries have a deliciously tart flavour that cuts through the sweetness of the dates in this energy-boosting snack. Many so-called healthy snack bars are high in added sugars and contain little protein. These simple-to-make slices give you a decent amount of fibre and protein to fill you up for longer.

RAW BRAZIL NUT, DATE AND CHERRY SLICE

150g/5½oz/1¼ cups Brazil nuts

150g/5½oz/1 heaped cup unsweetened dried cherries

200g/7oz/1¼ cups medjool dates, pitted

2 tbsp extra virgin coconut oil

MAKES 8 SLICES

- Line a shallow 23 × 15cm/9 × 6in baking pan with baking parchment.

- Put all the ingredients into a food processor and blend together. Press the mixture, which will be quite crumbly at this stage, into the prepared pan.

- Leave to set for 1 hour in the fridge. Cut into 8 slices and store in a sealed container in the fridge for up to 1 week. You can also freeze the slices in a sealed container for up to 2 weeks. To take to work, wrap in baking parchment, and keep cool, preferably next to an ice pack in your lunch box.

★ PACKED WITH . . .

Dried fruit is bursting with nutrients, but it also has a much higher concentration of sugar than a similar-size serving of fresh fruit, so don't overindulge. Combining the fruit with the healthy fats in the Brazil nuts and coconut oil allows a steady release of energy. This is a perfect pre-gym snack.

When you need a burst of energy to keep you going between meals, these no-cook balls are perfect. They are packed with protein and extremely easy to make. The ingredients might seem costly, but they will work out much cheaper in the long run than buying ready-made energy balls.

APRICOT AND CASHEW ENERGY BALLS

100g/3½oz/⅔ cup dried apricots

1 tbsp protein powder (such as hemp, sunflower or pea)

2 tbsp unsalted cashew nut butter

2 tbsp cashew nuts

½ tsp vanilla extract

1 tbsp honey

a pinch of sea salt

2 tbsp desiccated/dried shredded coconut

MAKES 10 BALLS

- Soak the apricots in boiling water for 2 minutes until softened, then drain well.

- Put all the ingredients, except the coconut, into a food processor and blend until well combined.

- Sprinkle the coconut onto a plate. Using your hands, roll the mixture into bite-size balls and then roll them into the coconut until well coated.

- Store in a sealed container in the fridge for up to 4 days. They can also be frozen for up to 3 months. To take to work, wrap individual balls in foil or baking parchment.

TIP When buying protein powder, read the label carefully and choose one with as few ingredients as possible – you don't want any added nasties such as unnatural additives or fillers.

 MAKE A CHANGE Try out other nuts you might have, such as hazelnuts, macadamia nuts and walnuts. Instead of desiccated/dried shredded coconut, you could also use chopped nuts, seeds or some raw cacao nibs.

★ PACKED WITH . . .

Cashew nuts are an excellent source of copper, a mineral that provides a helping hand in so many of our body processes, including energy production.

This is a delicious dairy- and guilt-free alternative to fudge. It really is full of healthy stuff and it's easy to make, with no cooking involved. They're so good for you that it's completely fine to eat three to four squares a day.

FEEL-GOOD SALTED PEANUT AND RAW CACAO FUDGE

125g/4½oz/¾ cup medjool dates, pitted

50g/1¾oz/¼ cup extra virgin coconut oil

4 tsp raw cacao powder

4 tbsp ground flaxseeds

6 tbsp unsalted, no-added-sugar peanut butter

a generous pinch of sea salt

MAKES ABOUT 30 SQUARES

- Soak the dates in boiling water for 5 minutes and then drain well. Put the coconut oil in a non-stick pan over a medium heat, and stir for 1 minute until melted.

- Meanwhile, line a 23cm × 15cm/9 × 6in shallow baking pan with baking parchment.

- Put the oil, dates and the remaining ingredients into a food processor and whizz until well combined and a dough is formed.

- Transfer the dough to the prepared pan and press down firmly until level. Put in the freezer for 1 hour until firm, and then cut into bite-size pieces, each about 2cm/¾in square.

- Store in a container in the freezer for up to 2 weeks. To take to work, wrap in baking parchment and cling film/plastic wrap or foil and keep cool, preferably next to an ice pack in your lunch box to avoid it becoming a little soggy – it's definitely worth this extra care.

⭐ PACKED WITH . . .

Both the fudges in the main recipe and the variation are packed with fibre, protein and healthy fats, as well as having the antioxidant and mood-enhancing benefits of raw cacao.

⬅ MAKE A CHANGE ➡ For Spiced Ginger and

Cacao Fudge, omit the peanut butter and sea salt, and replace with 25g/1oz/¼ cup walnuts, 2cm/¾in piece of root ginger, peeled and grated, 1 tsp mixed spice/apple pie spice and a pinch of sea salt.

INDEX

lettuce: Paleo breakfast 42
lunch boxes 14

M

mangoes: avocado, cucumber and mango salsa 144
  tuna and mango sushi rolls 161
matcha tea 27
mint and yogurt dip 158
miso 115
Monday morning chicken salad 48
muesli made easy 33
muffins: apricot muffins 41
  date and pecan spelt muffins 40
mushrooms: creamy wild mushroom soup 109
  mushroom, cashew and miso 115
  shiitake mushroom and cream cheese sushi
    rolls 161

N

noodles 114–15
  nutty noodle salad 81
  prawn tom yum soup 95
nori: sushi rolls 160–1
nuts 155
  good-for-you granola 35
  nutty noodle salad 81
  toasted nuts 97
  see also almonds, walnuts etc

O

oats: coconut, pistachio and goji berry granola
    bars 39
  date and pecan spelt muffins 40
  good mood cookies 179
  hot or cold overnight oats 30
  muesli made easy 33

quinoa, oats and chia porridge 32
oils: dressings 53
olives: sardine, tomato, olive and caper salad 63

P

Paleo breakfast 42
Paleo frittata 43
papaya: superfruit with matcha, yogurt and
    pistachios 27
paprika popcorn 176
Parmesan croûtons 97
pâté: trout, coconut and lime 128
peanuts: feel-good salted peanut and raw cacao
    fudge 185
pear, hazelnut and goat's cheese salad 65
peas: courgetti, pea and avocado salad pot 74
pecan nuts: date and pecan spelt muffins 40
peppers: avocado, cucumber and mango salsa 144
  beef brisket chilli 121
  Beluga lentils, roasted red pepper and feta salad
    77
  brain-booster salad pot 64
  chorizo, courgette and red pepper 115
  immune-boosting soup 106
  roasted red pepper hummus 142
  warm roast vegetable and halloumi salad 122
pesto 151
pickles 155
pine nuts: artichoke, spinach and pine nut dip 138
pistachio nuts: coconut, pistachio and goji berry
    granola bars 39
popcorn: paprika popcorn 176
  salted honey popcorn 176
porridge: quinoa, oats and chia 32

ACKNOWLEDGEMENTS

Huge thanks to the enthusiastic and talented publishing team at Nourish for bringing *Packed* to life. Special thanks to Rebecca Woods and Jo Lal for championing our idea in the first place, and to Becci for her amazing food styling skills. Liz, Max and Georgie brought such creativity to the photos; thank you – packed lunches never looked so good.

ABOUT THE AUTHORS

MICHELLE: I would like to thank my wonderful children Sophie and Jack and husband David, for all their support and for rigorously road-testing my lunch ideas.

BECKY: Thanks to Steve, Izzie and Polly for being such easy-going, helpful testers. Thanks also to our friends in St Albans, especially the commuters, who shared their lunch habits with us and said 'What a great idea'.

NOURISH
EAT WELL, LIVE WELL

Here at Nourish we're all about wellbeing through food and drink – irresistible dishes with a serious good-for-you factor. If you want to eat and drink delicious things that set you up for the day, suit any special diets, keep you healthy and make the most of the ingredients you have, we've got some great ideas to share with you. Come over to our blog for wholesome recipes and fresh inspiration – nourishbooks.com

BECKY ALEXANDER
is a food writer (The Guild of Food Writers) and editor for companies such as Dorling Kindersley, Vermilion, Bloomsbury and Nourish. She writes a fortnightly food column for *The Herts Advertiser* newspaper focusing on seasonal, local food. Becky has commuted for many years so has packed a lot of lunchboxes, and recently appeared on a BBC Radio programme giving commuters easy ideas for their lunches.

MICHELLE LAKE
(Dip ION CNHC mBANT) is a registered Nutritional Therapist. She has been running her own busy practice, Mission Nutrition, in St. Albans since 2007 and has provided countless clients from all walks of life with healthy and practical lunch solutions. She trained for four years at the Institute of Optimum Nutrition. Michelle is a member of BANT (British Association for Applied Nutrition and Nutritional Therapy) and The Complementary and Natural Healthcare Council (CNHC).